VEGAN MEAL PREP COOKBOOK FO   ....TES

100 HIGH PROTEIN, WHOLE FOOD, PLANT BASED RECIPES TO BUILD MUSCLES AND IMPROVE YOUR HEALTH

Joseph P. Turner

Copyright © All Right Reserved.

DISCLAIMER

The information provided in this program is for educational purposes only. The author is not a doctor and this information shouldn't be taken as medical advice. You should get a physician's approval before attempting any of the information in this program. This program is designed for healthy adults of 18 years and older. If you have any existing injuries, conditions or health issues, please seek your physician's approval before attempting any type of information in this program. The author is not liable or responsible for any damages, resulting from the use of this program. The user acknowledges any risk of injury, caused or alleged, with the use of this information. If your physician advises to not use the information provided in the program, please abide by those orders.

Always seek the advice of your physician or another qualified health provider with any questions you may have regarding a medical condition. Never disregard professional medical advice or delay seeking it because of something you have read here. Full medical clearance from a licensed physician should be obtained before beginning or modifying any diet, exercise, or lifestyle program, and your physician should be informed of all nutritional changes.

YOUR FREE GIFT

As a way of saying thanks for your purchase, I'm offering a free bonus book «**How Vegans Get Calcium, Iron, Zinc, Phosphorus, Vitamins A, B12, C & D: Mineral & Vitamin Deficiencies on a Vegan Diet and How to Fix Them**»

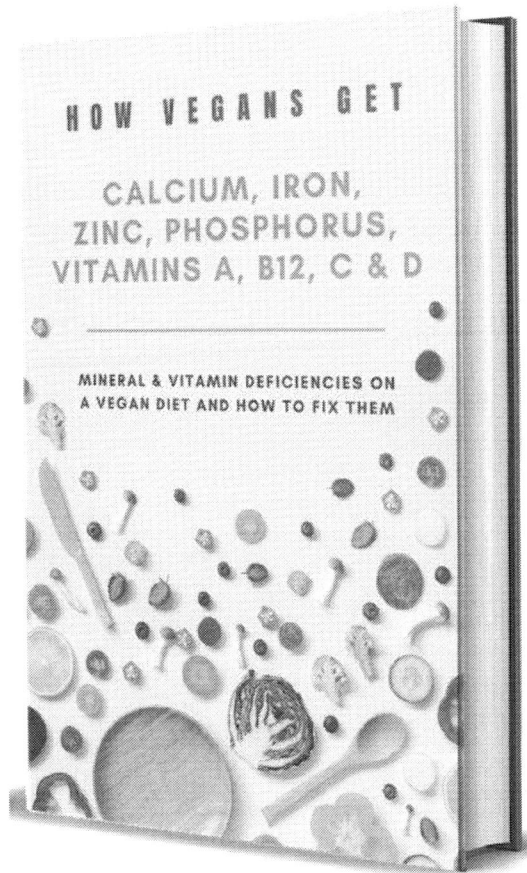

GET THE LINK AT THE END OF THE BOOK

TABLE OF CONTENTS

Meal Prep

Planning and preparing your meals ahead of time will make healthy choices an easy task, and it will link you with good dietary habits.

Having pre-prepared meals on hand can also choose a portion size and help you reach your nutrition goals.

Some researches found that one of the biggest barriers athletes report in their journey towards healthier eating is not having enough time in the day to cook or prepare meals.

Athletes have tight schedules, where they might be eating meals at strange hours, and sometimes get so busy that they are relying on bars and shakes for too many meals.

Follow These Meal Prep Tips:

✓ Write a Shopping list of all the ingredients you will need to buy to make the meals in your weekly plan. To have all in one place, we recommend downloading some shopping list applications or to create a shopping list with your Google Assistant on Google Home.
✓ Purchase the right containers, all kinds, and different shapes. The best choice is to purchase a glass or ceramic vessel refractory containers with locking lids. The best types of packaging for the freezer:
  • Ziploc Freezer Bags
  • Vacuum Sealer
  • Tupperware freezer containers

✓ Organize your time for cooking. If you are a busy person, seizure your weekend to get your meal prepping done, so you've got meals for the beginning of the week.
✓ Check grocery stores in your beforehand. Use Internet research for online grocery shopping; it saves your time and money.
✓ Use healthy cooking methods such as baking, steaming, broiling, grilling, and roasting.
✓ Instant Pot meal prep can make the week ahead a lot easier to deal with it.

Important Note: According to the Food and Drug Administration, after food is cooked, it should sit out at room temperature no more than two hours before being refrigerated or frozen!

How to Properly Reheat Your Refrigerated/Frozen Food?

  • Reheat sauces, soups, and gravies by bringing them to a rolling boil.
  • Cover your food to reheat; this retains moisture.
  • Put any foods that don't have much or any sauce (potatoes, steamed veggies) in stainless steel or cast-iron pan; reheat over medium-high heat.

- Pour the soup/stew into a microwave-safe container and heat the soup/stew on high for 20 to 30 seconds.
- **Do not reheat in the microwave oven**: Leafy greens, Chili peppers, fruits, Red pasta sauce, bread, Anything reheated before.

BREAKFAST

ALMOND QUEEN FRUIT SMOOTHIE

Ready in Time: 10 minutes | Servings: 2

Ingredients

1 1/2 cup almond milk

1 small peeled banana cut into 1-inch chunks and frozen

1 cup frozen peaches, sliced, thawed

3 Tbsp toasted almonds ground

1 scoop protein powder (pea or soy)

1 Tbsp flaxseed (ground)

Instructions

1. Add all ingredients into a high-speed blender and blend until smooth.

2. Pour your smoothie into the bottle, glass, or Mason jars; cover and keep refrigerated up to 2 days.

3. Or, pour your smoothie into a freezer-safe Ziploc bag and freeze up to 3 months.

4. Let it defrost in the refrigerator overnight, stir and enjoy!

Nutrition Facts

Percent daily values based on the Reference Daily Intake (RDI) for a 2000 calorie diet.

Amount Per Serving

Calories 262 | Calories From Fat (26%) 67.61 | Total Fat 8g 12% |

Saturated Fat 0.7g 3% | Cholesterol 1.16mg <1% | Sodium 26.49mg 1% | Potassium 497.5mg 14% | Total Carbohydrates 45.27g 15% |

Fiber 5.6g 21% | Sugar 34.85g | Protein 6.58g 13%

Baked Raisins & Pumpkin Energy Bars

Ready in time: 35 minutes | Servings: 8

Ingredients

1 Tbsp olive oil for greasing

1 tsp pure vanilla extract

1/2 cup of applesauce

1 1/2 cups of rolled oats

2/3 cup golden raisins

1/2 cup of toasted hazelnuts, chopped

1/2 cup of pumpkin seeds

2 tsp vegan protein powder (e.g., chia, soy or hemp)

1/4 tsp cinnamon

1/2 tsp ginger

Pinch of salt to taste

Instructions

1. Preheat the oven to 350 F.

2. Grease a square baking dish.

3. Stir the vanilla extract and applesauce in a large.

4. Stir the oats into the applesauce mixture.

5. Add all remaining ingredients and stir until thoroughly combined.

6. Spoon mixture into the prepared baking dish and press down until even.

7. Place into oven and bake for about 25 minutes.

8. Remove from the oven, and allow it to cool down completely.

9. Slice into 16 small (or eight large) square or rectangle bars.

10. Wrap each bar with the paper and store at room temperature for up to 3 weeks.

11. Also, you can freeze your energy bars in airtight container or freezer bag to keep it fresh for longer.

Nutrition Facts

Percent daily values based on the Reference Daily Intake (RDI) for a 2000 calorie diet.

Amount Per Serving

Calories 279.13 | Calories From Fat (39%) 109.62 | % Daily Value | Total Fat 12.3g 20% | Saturated Fat 1.24g 6% | Cholesterol 0.19mg <1% | Sodium 303.7mg 13% | Potassium 318.72mg 9% | Total Carbohydrates 38.1g 13% | Fiber 4.16g 17% | Sugar 16.48g | Protein 6g 11%

BAKED SAVORY OAT-APPLE BARS

Ready in Time: 45 minutes | Servings: 8

Ingredients

1 Tbs sesame oil (or olive oil)

2 tart apples grated

1/2 cup Instant oats

1/2 cup of Rolled oats

1 cup oat flour

1/4 tsp salt

1 tsp baking powder

3/4 cup of dates

2/3 cup sesame butter or tahini

3 Tbsp Chia seeds

1/2 cup of almond milk

1 tsp pure vanilla extract

Instructions

1. Preheat oven to 350 F.

2. Grease a 9×9" baking pan with oil.

3. Peel and grate apples; place in a colander to drain.

4. In a large bowl, combine Instant and Rolled oats, oat flour, salt, and baking powder.

5. In a separate bowl, stir drained apple, dates, sesame butter, Chia seeds, almond milk, and vanilla extract until everything is combined well (use a mixer).

6. Add apple mixture to the oat mixture and stir until all ingredients are well incorporated

7. Place the batter into a prepared baking pan.

8. Place in the oven, and bake for 30 minutes.

9. Remove pan from the oven, and let cool completely before slicing.

10. Store bars in a sealed container at room temperature for up to 4 days or refrigerate up to one week.

Nutrition Facts

Percent daily values based on the Reference Daily Intake (RDI) for a 2000 calorie diet.

Amount Per Serving

Calories 316 | Calories From Fat (41%) 130.2 | Total Fat 15.8g 24% | Saturated Fat 2.1g 11% | Cholesterol 0mg 0% | Sodium 208mg 9% | Potassium 353.85mg 10% | Total Carbohydrates 41.74g 14% | Fiber 7.16g 29% | Sugar 16g | Protein 7.62g 15%

BOOSTING CELERY-COCONUT SMOOTHIE

Ready in Time: 10 minutes | Servings: 2

Ingredients

2 celery stalks, chopped

3 cup kale leaves, fresh and chopped

1 large banana cut into slices

1 1/2 cup coconut milk (canned)

1 Tbsp protein powder (pea or soy)

1 Tbsp lemon juice

1 Tbsp chia seeds

Instructions

1. Add all ingredients in your blender and blend until smooth.

2. Pour your smoothie into the bottle, glass, or Mason jars; cover and keep refrigerated up to 2 days.

3. Or, pour your smoothie into a freezer-safe Ziploc bag and freeze up to 3 months.

4. Let it defrost in the refrigerator overnight, stir and enjoy!

Nutrition Facts

Percent daily values based on the Reference Daily Intake (RDI) for a 2000 calorie diet.

Amount Per Serving

Calories 473.21 | Calories From Fat (70%) 333.57 | Total Fat 39.7g 61% | Saturated Fat 32.49g 162% | Cholesterol 1.16mg <1% | Sodium 89mg 4% | Potassium 926.64mg 26% | Total Carbohydrates 28.8g 10% | Fiber 6.1g 24% | Sugar 9.5g | Protein 9.2g 18%

Breakfast Potato Patties

Ready in Time: 45 minutes Servings: 8

Ingredients

1 1/2 lb grated potatoes

1 grated onion

3 Tbsp applesauce unsweetened (canned)

Salt and ground black pepper to taste

2 Tbsp all-purpose flour

1/2 cup olive or canola oil for frying

Instructions

1. Add all ingredients In a large bowl, and stir until all ingredients combined well.

2. Form the batter into flat patties.

3. Heat oil in a large frying skillet over medium heat.

4. Fry your potato patties for about 6 to 7 minutes, and then flip with a spatula and fry from the other side until done.

5. Remove ready patties on a plate lined with kitchen paper to drain, and completely cool.

6. Transfer your patties in a single layer to baking sheets.

7. Freeze patties until hard.

8. Transfer the frozen patties to freezer bags and keep in freeze up to 2 weeks.

9. Reheat in a microwave oven.

Nutrition Facts

Percent daily values based on the Reference Daily Intake (RDI) for a 2000 calorie diet.

Amount Per Serving

Calories 201.55 | Calories From Fat (60%) 121.42 | Total Fat 13.74g 21% | Saturated Fat 1g 5% | Cholesterol 0mg 0% | Sodium 5.87mg <1% | Potassium 386.69mg 11% | Total Carbohydrates 18.2g 6% | Fiber 2.25g 9% | Sugar 1.5g | Protein 2.8g 6%

CARROT 'CAKE' SMOOTHIE

Ready in Time: 10 minutes | Servings: 2

Ingredients

2 grated carrots

2 cups almond milk

4 Tbs rolled oats

1 orange, juiced (about 1/2 cup)

1 Tbsp chia seeds

3/4 tsp cinnamon

1 Tbsp protein powder (pea or soy)

1/2 tsp vanilla extract

Instructions

1. Add all the ingredients to your high-speed blender and blend on high until completely smooth.

2. If your smoothie is too thick, add some more almond milk.

3. Pour your smoothie into the bottle, glass, or Mason jars; cover and keep refrigerated up to 2 days.

4. Or, pour your smoothie into a freezer-safe Ziploc bag and freeze up to 3 months.

5. Let it defrost in the refrigerator overnight, stir and enjoy!

Nutrition Facts

Percent daily values based on the Reference Daily Intake (RDI) for a 2000 calorie diet.

Amount Per Serving

Calories 191.11 | Calories From Fat (21%) 40.41 | Total Fat 4.6g 7% |

Saturated Fat 0.59g 3% | Cholesterol 1.16mg <1% | Sodium 76.26mg 3% | Potassium 507.62mg 15% | Total Carbohydrates 30.18g 10% | Fiber 8g 32% | Sugar 7.1g | Protein 8.41g 16%

Carrot, Almond and Dill Muffins

Ready in Time: 45 minutes | Servings: 12

Ingredients

2 cups of pastry flour

2 tsp baking powder

4 Tbsp almond meal

2 Tbsp brown sugar

Pinch of salt

2 tsp fresh dill, finely chopped

1 small ripe banana mashed

1 cup of carrots, grated

3 cup almond milk

1 cup olive oil

1/4 cup apple-sauce unsweetened

2 Tbsp extracted honey

Instructions

1. Preheat oven to 375 F.

2. Grease 12 muffin cups; set aside.

3. Combine pastry flour with the baking powder, almond meal, sugar, carrot, banana, dill, and salt.

4. In a separate bowl, beat the almond milk, applesauce, and honey with a hand mixer.

5. Slowly, add the milk mixture to the flour mixture and beat until combined well.

6. Divide the mixture into the prepared muffin cups (3/4 of a cup).

7. Bake for about 30 to 35 minutes or until a toothpick inserted inside comes out clean.

8. Remove from the oven, and allow to cool completely,

9. Store your muffins in an airtight container; it will last up to 3 days at room temperature or seven days in the fridge.

Nutrition Facts

Percent daily values based on the Reference Daily Intake (RDI) for a 2000 calorie diet.

Amount Per Serving

Calories 108.14 | Calories From Fat (2%) 2.27 | Total Fat 0.27g <1% | Saturated Fat 0.05g <1% | Cholesterol 0mg 0% | Sodium 89.22mg 4% | Potassium 99.35mg 3% | Total Carbohydrates 24.5g 8% | Fiber 1.5g 5% | Sugar 6.49g | Protein 2.69g 6%

DARK CACAO BANANA MUFFINS

Ready in Time: 28 minutes | Servings: 12

Ingredients

non- stick baking spray

1/2 cup coconut butter softened

1 cup light brown sugar (packed)

4 Tbsp applesauce

2 bananas mashed

3 Tbsp coconut milk (canned)

2 cups of wheat flour all-purposed

1 tsp baking soda

Pinch of sea salt

1/3 cup cacao dry powder, unsweetened

1 cup toasted walnuts, chopped

1 cup water for Instant Pot

Instructions

1. Grease12 muffin cups (ceramic or silicon) with non-stick spray; set aside.

2. Add softened coconut butter and brown sugar in a mixing bowl.

3. Beat with an electric mixer until smooth and combined well.

4. Add the applesauce, banana, and coconut milk; continue to beat for the further 30 seconds.

5. Add in the flour, salt, and baking soda; beat on medium speed until all ingredients combined well.

6. Add the cacao powder and toasted walnuts; reduce speed to low, and continue to mix until combined well.

7. Pour the batter into prepared muffin cups.

8. Pour water to the inner stainless steel pot of your Instant Pot, and place the trivet inside.

9. Place muffin cups onto the trivet.

10. Lock lid into place and set on the MANUAL setting high pressure for 18 minutes.

11. Use the Quick Release valve to let the pressure out.

12. Remove muffins from the pot and allow to cool down completely.

13. Place muffins in a plastic bag, and store at room temperature for up to 3 days.

14. Or, place muffins into freezer bags and freeze for up to 3 months.

15. Before consuming, reheat your muffins in the microwave .

16. Microwave on HIGH about 30 seconds for each muffin.

Nutrition Facts

Percent daily values based on the Reference Daily Intake (RDI) for a 2000 calorie diet.

Amount Per Serving

Calories 320 | Calories From Fat (45%) 143.21 | Total Fat 16.84g 26% | Saturated Fat 9.41g 47% | Cholesterol 0mg 0% | Sodium 208.81mg 9% | Potassium 208.48mg 6% | Total Carbohydrates 41.77g 14% | Fiber 2.58g 10% | Sugar 21g | Protein 5.43g 10%

Darkwood Coconut Smoothie

Ready in Time: 10 minutes | Servings: 2

Ingredients

1 cup of fresh coconut meat finely chopped/sliced

1 1/2 cups of coconut milk

2 Tbsp of coconut butter

1 avocado (peeled, diced)

3 Tbsp cacao powder

2 tsp of cinnamon

1 scoop vegan protein powder (pea or soy protein)

1 Tbsp chia seeds

3 Tbsp strained or extracted honey

Instructions

1. Add all ingredients into a high-speed blender and blend until smooth.

2. Pour your smoothie into the bottle, glass, or Mason jars; cover and keep refrigerated up to 2 days.

3. Or, pour your smoothie into a freezer-safe Ziploc bag and freeze up to 3 months.

4. Let it defrost in the refrigerator overnight, stir and enjoy!

Nutrition Facts

Percent daily values based on the Reference Daily Intake (RDI) for a 2000 calorie diet.

Amount Per Serving

Calories 555.37 | Calories From Fat (38%) 389.16 | Total Fat 43.84g 74% | Saturated Fat 25.6g 70% | Cholesterol 0mg 0% | Sodium 50.22mg 2% | Potassium 1226.85mg 35% | Total Carbohydrates 61g 21% | Fiber 22.18g 89% | Sugar 27.7g | Protein 13.24g 26%

Delicious Seasoned Tomato Bread

Ready in Time: 45 minutes | Servings: 8

Ingredients

1 1/2 cups plain white flour

1 cup almond flour

1/2 tsp baking powder

1/2 tsp baking soda

1/2 tsp salt

1 1/2 tsp garlic powder

1 tsp dried onion powder

1 Tbsp dried basil

1/2 tsp dried oregano

4 Tbsp olive oil

3 Tbsp soy milk or almond milk

1 1/2 cups of pureed tomatoes (canned)

2 1/2 Tbsp tomato paste

1 Tbsp soy sauce

Instructions

1. Preheat your oven to 360 F.

2. Grease a loaf pan with olive oil; set aside.

3. Stir flours, baking powder and soda, salt, garlic, and onion powder, basil, and oregano in a large bowl.

4. In a separate bowl, stir all wet ingredients.

5. Fold the wet ingredients into the flour mixture, and stir until very well combined.

6. Pour the batter into a prepared baking loaf.

7. Bake for 35 minutes or until a toothpick inserted into the center comes out clean.

8. Remove from the oven and allow to cool down completely in the loaf pan.

9. Cover with a kitchen towel.

10. Cut the bread into slices, store into a container, and keep up to 3 days at room temperature.

11. Or, wrap bread slices, add into freezer bags, and freeze for longer-term storage.

12. Defrost a tomato bread slices; microwave them on high power for 20 to 25 seconds.

Nutrition Facts

Percent daily values based on the Reference Daily Intake (RDI) for a 2000 calorie diet.

Amount Per Serving

Calories 265.18 | Calories From Fat (52%) 137.72 | Total Fat 16.08g 25% | Saturated Fat 1.7g 8% | Cholesterol 0mg 0% | Sodium 428,05mg 18% | Potassium 314mg 9% | Total Carbohydrates 25.5g 9% | Fiber 3.54g 14% | Sugar 2.69g | Protein 7g 14%

FROZEN BERRIES VIGOR SMOOTHIE

Ready in Time: 10 minutes | Servings: 2

Ingredients

1 1/2 cups almond milk

3/4 cup frozen berries, thawed (any)

1/2 cup fresh spinach leaves chopped

1 large banana sliced

3 Tbsp peanut butter

2 Tbsp strained honey

1 scoop vegan protein powder (soy)

Instructions

1. Add all ingredients in your blender, and blend until combined well.

2. Pour your smoothie into the bottle, glass, or Mason jars; cover and keep refrigerated up to 2 days.

3. Or, pour your smoothie into a freezer-safe Ziploc bag and freeze up to 3 months.

4. Let it defrost in the refrigerator overnight, stir and enjoy!

Nutrition Facts

Percent daily values based on the Reference Daily Intake (RDI) for a 2000 calorie diet.

Amount Per Serving

Calories 301 | Calories From Fat (38%) 113.68 | Total Fat 13.52g 21% | Saturated Fat 2.71g 14% | Cholesterol 1.16mg <1% | Sodium 137mg 6% | Potassium 570.22mg 16% | Total Carbohydrates 41.18g 14% | Fiber 4.72g 19% | Sugar 29.82g | Protein 10g 20%

GREEN QUINOA BREAKFAST PATTIES

Ready in Time: 20 minutes | Servings: 4

Ingredients

1 1/2 cup cooked quinoa

1/2 cup shredded carrots

1/2 cup shredded carrots

2 Tbsp flaxseed (soaked in 6 Tbsp water)

1/2 cup plain bread crumbs

2 garlic cloves minced

1 tsp onion powder

1 tsp garlic powder

2 Tbsp fresh parsley finely chopped

Salt and ground black pepper to taste

2 Tbsp extra virgin olive oil (plus additional for cooking)

Olive oil for frying

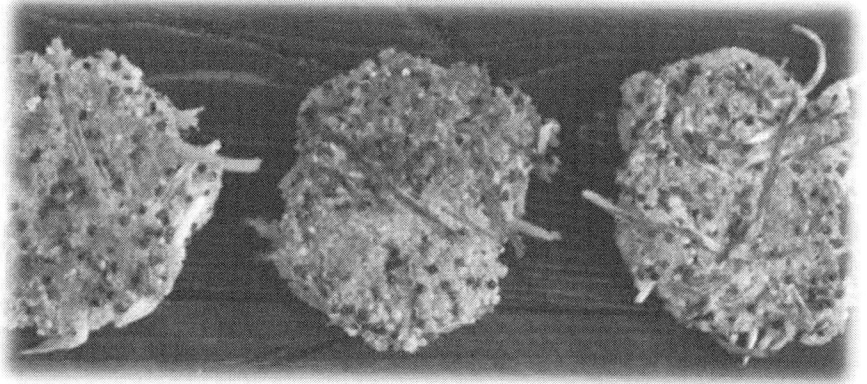

Instructions

1. In a large bowl, combine all ingredients until combined well.

2. Make patties out of the mixture.

3. Heat oil in a non-stick frying skillet.

4. Fry quinoa patties on both sides 2-3 minutes or until crisp.

5. Drain on a plate lined with a paper towel.

6. Keep refrigerated in an airtight container for up to 5 days.

Nutrition Facts

Percent daily values based on the Reference Daily Intake (RDI) for a 2000 calorie diet.

Amount Per Serving

Calories 155.38 | Calories From Fat (12%) 19.11 | Total Fat 2.15g 3% | Saturated Fat 0.18g <1% | Cholesterol 0mg 0% | Sodium 124.87mg 5% | Potassium 265.48mg 8% | Total Carbohydrates 28.8g 10% | Fiber 3.58g 14% | Sugar 2.23g | Protein 5.45g 11%

HIGH PROTEIN CHIA AND BANANA SMOOTHIE

Ready in Time: 10 minutes | Servings: 2

Ingredients

1 1/2 cup of coconut milk (canned)

2 Tbsp peanut butter, unsweetened

2 Tbsp chia seeds

1 cup celery leaves, finely chopped

1 large banana, sliced

1 scoop vegan protein powder (pea or soy protein)

2 Tbsp dark honey strained

Instructions

1. Add all ingredients into high-speed blender; blend until smooth and combined well.

2. Pour your smoothie into the bottle, glass, or Mason jars; cover and keep refrigerated up to 2 days.

3. Or, pour your smoothie into a freezer-safe Ziploc bag and freeze up to 3 months.

4. Let it defrost in the refrigerator overnight, stir and enjoy!

Nutrition Facts

Percent daily values based on the Reference Daily Intake (RDI) for a 2000 calorie diet.

Amount Per Serving

Calories 620,1 | Calories From Fat (66%) 406.92 | Total Fat 48.55g 75% | Saturated Fat 34.23g 171% | Cholesterol 1.16mg <1% | Sodium 129.3mg 5% | Potassium 861.45mg 25% | Total Carbohydrates 44.64g 15% | Fiber 7g 28% | Sugar 26.32g | Protein 12.68g 25%

ICED SALAD AND PINEAPPLE SMOOTHIE

Ready in Time: 10 minutes | Servings: 2

Ingredients

1 1/2 cups soy milk

2 Tbsp almond butter (plain, unsalted)

1 small head of lettuce chopped

1 cup raw pineapple chunks

1 large banana, cut into 1-inch pieces

1 scoop vegan protein powder (e.g., chia, soy or hemp)

2 Tbsp maple syrup

1 cup iced cubes (optional)

Instructions

1. Combine all ingredients in a blender and blend until smooth.

2. Pour your smoothie into the bottle, glass, or Mason jars; cover and keep refrigerated up to 2 days.

3. Or, pour your smoothie into a freezer-safe Ziploc bag and freeze up to 3 months.

4. Let it defrost in the refrigerator overnight, stir and enjoy!

Nutrition Facts

Percent daily values based on the Reference Daily Intake (RDI) for a 2000 calorie diet.

Amount Per Serving

Calories 368.7 | Calories From Fat (31%) 114.44 | Total Fat 13.36g 21% | Saturated Fat 1.2g 6% | Cholesterol 1.16mg <1% | Sodium 118.73mg 5% | Potassium 779.15mg 22% | Total Carbohydrates 54g 18% | Fiber 6.15g 25% | Sugar 36.27g | Protein 13.7g 28%

DRIED FRUIT ENERGY BARS

Ready in Time: 10 minutes | Servings: 4

Ingredients

1 cup dried plums chopped

1 cup pitted raisins

1 cup dried apricots chopped

3 Tbsp lemon juice

1 handful of chia seeds

2 Tbsp extracted honey

Instructions

1. Add all ingredients in your food processor; process it until getting a smooth mixture.

2. Apply the mixture in a baking sheet, and flat with a spatula; refrigerate the mixture for 2 hours.

3. Cut the mixture into bars.

4. Keep your energy bars tightly covered in the Ziploc bag in the refrigerator or freezer.

Nutrition Facts

Percent daily values based on the Reference Daily Intake (RDI) for a 2000 calorie diet.

Amount Per Serving

Calories 280.9 | Calories From Fat (2%) 4.23 | Total Fat 0.51g <1% | Saturated Fat 0.04g <1% | Cholesterol 0mg 0% | Sodium 12.61mg <1% | Potassium 900.12mg 26% | Total Carbohydrates 74.15g 25% | Fiber 5.9g 24% | Sugar 46.38g | Protein 3.1g 6%

SAVORY STORM WHITE SMOOTHIE

Ready in Time: 15 minutes | Servings: 2

Ingredients

2 cups steamed cauliflower florets

Pinch of salt

1 1/2 cups coconut milk (canned)

1 medium banana sliced

1 scoop vegan protein powder (pea, chia or soy protein)

2 Tbsp agave syrup or honey

Instructions

1. Rinse, clean and steam cauliflower florets with a pinch of salt for about 5 to 6 minutes; drain.

2. Add cauliflower into a high-speed blender along with all remaining ingredients.

3. Blend until smooth.

4. Pour your smoothie into the bottle, glass, or Mason jars; cover and keep refrigerated up to 2 days.

5. Or, pour your smoothie into a freezer-safe Ziploc bag and freeze up to 3 months.

6. Let it defrost in the refrigerator overnight, stir and enjoy!

Nutrition Facts

Percent daily values based on the Reference Daily Intake (RDI) for a 2000 calorie diet.

Amount Per Serving

Calories 486 | Calories From Fat (65%) 315.23 | Total Fat 37.58g 58% | Saturated Fat 32.28g 161% | Cholesterol 1.16mg <1% | Sodium 73.12mg 3% | Potassium 987.62mg 28% | Total Carbohydrates 37.63g 13% | Fiber 4g 16% | Sugar 21.53g | Protein 8.71g 18%

SIMPLE VEGAN WAFFLES

Ready in Time: 20 minutes | Servings: 4

Ingredients

1 1/2 cups whole wheat flour (of any GF flour)

2 Tbs natural brown sugar

1 tsp baking soda

1 tsp baking powder

pinch of salt

1 tsp of protein powder

1 1/2 cups of almond milk

4 Tbsp virgin olive oil

Instructions

1. First, preheat your waffle maker according to manufacturers instructions.

2. Combine all ingredients in a bowl and stir until combine well.

3. Pour the half of the cup of batter in the center of the waffle maker.

4. Close the cover and wait until the light turns green.

5. Remove waffles on the warm plate and cover with kitchen paper.

6. Repeat this process with the rest of the batter.

7. Store waffles in an airtight container in refrigerate up to 3 days.

8. Or freeze your waffles in a freezer-safe bag/s up to two months.

9. Reheat your waffles in the oven at 350 F for 10 to 15 minutes.

Nutrition Facts

Percent daily values based on the Reference Daily Intake (RDI) for a 2000 calorie diet.

Amount Per Serving

Calories 230.38 | Calories From Fat (11%) 25.51 | Total Fat 2.49g 4% | Saturated Fat 0.09g <1% | Cholesterol 0.19mg <1% | Sodium 547.43mg 23% | Potassium 69.8mg 2% | Total Carbohydrates 44.13g 15% | Fiber 1.33g 5% | Sugar 6.85g | Protein 6g 12%

SPICY VEGAN BREAKFAST SMOOTHIE

Ready in Time: 10 minutes | Servings: 2

Ingredients

1 large banana sliced

1/2 cup of kale

1 cup of apple juice

1/2 cup of frozen berries (any)

2 to 3 Tbs almond butter

1/2 tsp grated ginger

1/2 tsp turmeric

1/4 tsp of cinnamon

1/4 tsp of cumin

1 scoop vegan protein powder (e.g., chia, soy or hemp)

Instructions

1. Add all ingredients in your blender; blend until smooth well.

2. Pour your smoothie into the bottle, glass, or Mason jars; cover and keep refrigerated up to 2 days.

3. Or, pour your smoothie into a freezer-safe Ziploc bag and freeze up to 3 months.

4. Let it defrost in the refrigerator overnight, stir and enjoy!

Nutrition Facts

Percent daily values based on the Reference Daily Intake (RDI) for a 2000 calorie diet.

Amount Per Serving

Calories 276.3 | Calories From Fat (42%) 115.16 | Total Fat 13.11g 20% | Saturated Fat 7.5g 38% | Cholesterol 31.69mg 11% | Sodium 29.82mg 1% | Potassium 583.68mg 17% | Total Carbohydrates 37.47g 13% | Fiber 4.34g 17% | Sugar 27.43g | Protein 4.72g 10%

TOTAL ALMOND & GINGER PEAR CAKE

Ready in Time: 45 minutes | Servings: 12

Ingredients

1 Tbsp avocado or olive oil

2 cups all-purpose flour

1 cup granulated sugar

1 1/2 tsp baking powder

1 Tbsp ground ginger

Pinch of salt

1/2 cup almond butter (plain, unsalted)

2 large pears cut into small dices

1/2 cup almonds, toasted and roughly chopped

2/3 cup almond milk

1 Tbsp applesauce canned

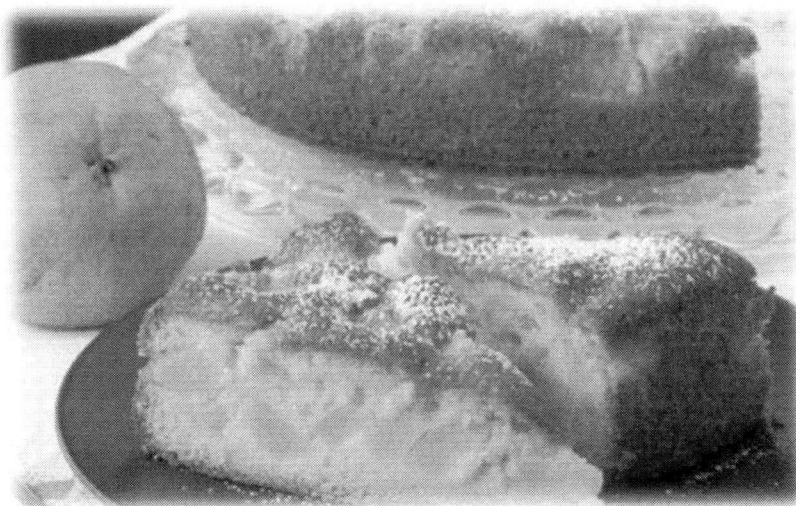

Instructions

1. Heat oven to 360 F.

2. Grease a baking dish with oil and set aside.

3. In a large bowl, stir flour and all dry ingredients.

4. Add almond butter and pears, and stir well.

5. Add all remaining ingredients and beat with a mixer on low until well combined.

6. Pour mixture into prepared baking dish.

7. Bake cake for 30 to 35 minutes or until a skewer inserted into the middle comes out almost clean.

8. Remove cake to a wire rack to completely cool.

9. Cut cake and store in an airtight container; keep

10. Keep it in a cool place for two days or refrigerate up to 5 days.

Nutrition Facts

Percent daily values based on the Reference Daily Intake (RDI) for a 2000 calorie diet.

Amount Per Serving

Calories 294 | Calories From Fat (29%) 85.7 | Total Fat 10.2g 16% | Saturated Fat 0.86g 4% | Cholesterol 0mg 0% | Sodium 160.12mg 7% | Potassium 230.36mg 7% | Total Carbohydrates 47.6g 16% | Fiber 4.56g 18% | Sugar 24.8g | Protein 5.83g 12%

Vegan Spinach Artichoke Quiche with Tofu

Ready in Time: 1 hour and 5 minutes | Servings: 6

Ingredients

2 large tortillas (gluten-free if needed)

non-stick cooking olive oil spray

2 Tbsp olive oil

1 small onion chopped

2 cloves of garlic minced

Salt and ground black pepper to taste

2 cups of fresh spinach

1 cup of soft tofu

4 Tbsp nutritional yeast

1 Tbsp yellow mustard

1 lemon juiced

1 tsp fresh parsley finely chopped

1 tsp fresh basil finely chopped

1 can (14 oz) artichoke hearts drained and chopped

Instructions

1. Preheat oven to 350 F.

2. Grease a baking pie dish with non-stick olive oil spray.

3. Chop tortillas and cover the baking dish evenly; sprinkle with some oil and set aside.

4. Heat olive oil in a frying skillet over medium-high heat.

5. Saute the onion and garlic with the pinch salt and pepper until soft or for about 3 to 4 minutes.

6. Add spinach and cook, occasionally stirring, for further 3 minutes or until spinach is wilted.

7. Remove from the heat and set aside.

8. Add tofu, nutritional yeast, mustard, lemon juice, parsley, and basil into a food processor; process until smooth and well combined.

9. Add artichoke hearts, and the onion mixture and process until combined well.

10. Pour artichoke mixture into a prepared baking dish with tortillas.

11. Bake for 40 to 45 minutes.

12. Remove from the oven and allow it to cool down completely.

13. Wrap a baking dish into aluminum foil and keep refrigerated up to 3 or 4 days.

14. If you slice your quiche, place individual slices into resealable plastic bags.

15. If you want to freeze your quiche, place the whole quiche into a freezer bag, and keep up to 1 month.

16. When you want to eat your quiche, reheat it in a pre-heated oven on 350 F for about 30 minutes.

Nutrition Facts

Percent daily values based on the Reference Daily Intake (RDI) for a 2000 calorie diet.

Amount Per Serving

Calories 130.2 | Calories From Fat (43%) 55.79 | Total Fat 6.41g 10% | Saturated Fat 0.83g 4% | Cholesterol 0mg 0% | Sodium 107mg 4% | Potassium 441.24mg 13% | Total Carbohydrates 14.54g 5% | Fiber 6.58g 26% | Sugar 1.27g | Protein 7.82g 16%

LUNCH

AROMATIC SPINACH WITH BASIL-SESAME PUREE

Ready in Time: 30 minutes | Servings: 4

Ingredients

1 lb fresh spinach

4 Tbsp of olive oil

1 onion finely chopped

1 leek finely chopped

3 cloves garlic

3 cup of vegetable broth

4 Tbsp grated tomato

1 cup fresh basil finely chopped

1/3 cup sesame oil

Salt and ground pepper to taste

Instructions

1. Boil spinach in salted water for 3 to 5 minutes.

2. Remove from heat and place in colander to drain.

3. Heat oil in a frying skillet over medium-high heat.

4. Sauté the onion, leek, and garlic with a pinch of salt, often stirring, for about 5 to 6 minutes.

5. Pour vegetable broth, grated tomato, and basil leaves; stir for 2 minutes.

6. Add spinach, give a good stir, cover, and cook for 6 - 8 minutes over medium-low heat.

7. Transfer the spinach mixture in a blender, and add the sesame oil; blend for 30 seconds or until smooth.

8. Taste and adjust salt and pepper.

9. Store in an airtight container and freeze for a month.

Nutrition Facts

Percent daily values based on the Reference Daily Intake (RDI) for a 2000 calorie diet.

Amount Per Serving

Calories 381.85 | Calories From Fat (77%) 295.2 | Total Fat 33.53g 52% | Saturated Fat 4.68g 23% | Cholesterol 0.46mg <1% | Sodium 843.36mg 35% | Potassium 552.58mg 16% | Total Carbohydrates 17.7g 6% | Fiber 6g 24% | Sugar 3.14g | Protein 6.76g 14%

BAKED QUINOA AND BLACK BEANS PATTIES

Ready in Time: 1 hour and 5 minutes | Servings: 2

Ingredients

1 cup of quinoa

1 cup of water

1 can (15 oz) of black beans

4 Tbsp sesame seeds

4 Tbsp bread crumbs

2 Tbsp tomato paste

1 Tbsp hot sauce (any)

2 Tbsp nutritional yeast

1 tsp garlic powder

1/2 tsp of oregano

1/2 tsp of rosemary

1 Tbsp fresh basil finely chopped

Salt and ground black pepper to taste

Instructions

1. In a pot, cook quinoa for about 15 minutes.

2. Place in a colander, and drain; let quinoa to cool down.

3. Preheat oven to 400 F.

4. Line a baking sheet with baking paper.

5. In a bowl, add black beans and mash with a fork.

6. Add quinoa, sesame seeds, and all remaining ingredients; stir until combine well.

7. Roll dough into balls.

8. Place quinoa balls/patties on a prepared baking sheet.

9. Bake for about 35 minutes.

10. Remove from the oven, and allow to cool completely.

11. Store in an airtight container and keep refrigerated up to 4 to 5 days.

Yield: 4 large patties

Nutrition Facts

Percent daily values based on the Reference Daily Intake (RDI) for a 2000 calorie diet.

Amount Per Serving

Calories 614,39 | Calories From Fat (21%) 130,31 | Total Fat 15.29g 24% | Saturated Fat 2.51g 13% | Cholesterol 0.21mg <1% | Sodium 719.14mg 30% | Potassium 1312.62mg 39% | Total Carbohydrates 93.57g 31% | Fiber 25g 100% | Sugar 5.48g | Protein 32g 64%

Barley and Broccoli Pilaf

Ready in Time: 55 minutes | Servings: 4

Ingredients

4 Tbsp olive oil

1 onion, chopped

salt and fresh ground pepper to taste

1 cup pearled barley

2 cups of vegan vegetable broth

1 cup of water

1 tsp fresh thyme

1 1/2 cup broccoli florets, cut into small pieces

1/4 cup green peas

1 carrot finely sliced

1 tomato sliced

Instructions

1. Heat oil in a large frying pan; sauté onion with a pinch of salt for 2 to 3 minutes.

2. Add barley and constantly stir for a further 2 minutes.

3. Add vegetable broth, thyme, and water and bring to boil.

4. Cover, reduce heat to low and simmer for 30 minutes.

5. Add all remaining ingredients, stir well, and cook for further 20 minutes.

6. Taste and adjust the salt and pepper to taste.

7. Allow it to cool completely.

8. Store barley pilaf in an airtight container and keep refrigerated up to 5 days.

9. Or, place in freezer bags and keep in the freezer for one month.

Nutrition Facts

Percent daily values based on the Reference Daily Intake (RDI) for a 2000 calorie diet.

Amount Per Serving

Calories 409.46 | Calories From Fat (37%) 151.2 | Total Fat 17.15g 26% | Saturated Fat 2.51g 13% | Cholesterol 0.62mg <1% | Sodium 635.47mg 26% | Potassium 588.46mg 17% | Total Carbohydrates 58.38g 19% | Fiber 11.61g 46% | Sugar 5.36g | Protein 8.63g 17%

Cabbage and Cauliflower Puree

Ready in Time: 30 minutes | Servings: 4

Ingredients

water for cooking

1/2 medium head cabbage

1/2 lb cauliflower florets

1 leek finely sliced

2 stalks fresh celery chopped

4 Tbsp olive oil

Salt and pepper to taste

Instructions

1. Heat water (about 4 1/2 cups) in a big pot and add all vegetables and oil; season with the little salt.

2. Bring to boil, reduce heat to medium, cover, and cook for about 15 -20 minutes.

3. Transfer vegetables in a blender; blend until smooth and combined well.

4. Taste and adjust the salt and pepper to taste.

5. Store in an airtight container and keep refrigerated up to 3 to 4 days.

Nutrition Facts

Percent daily values based on the Reference Daily Intake (RDI) for a 2000 calorie diet.

Amount Per Serving

Calories 176.15 | Calories From Fat (69%) 122.33 | Total Fat 13.85g 21% | Saturated Fat 2g 10% | Cholesterol 0mg 0% | Sodium 43.22mg 2% | Potassium 413.19mg 12% | Total Carbohydrates 12.7g 4% | Fiber 4.43g 18% | Sugar 5.6g | Protein 3g 6%

DARK RED VEGAN SOUP

Ready in Time: 1 hour and 10 minutes | Servings: 4

Ingredients

4 Tbsp olive oil

1 onion finely diced

2 cloves garlic finely chopped

salt and freshly ground black pepper

1 lb tomatoes, peeled and grated

2 beets, large, peeled and cut into pieces

2 carrots cut into strips

3/4 tsp cumin

1 tsp cayenne pepper

4 cups of vegetable broth

Instructions

1. Heat the oil in a large pot on medium-high temperature.

2. Add the onion and garlic and sauté with the pinch of salt, often stirring, for about 3 to 4 minutes.

3. Add grated tomatoes, beets, and carrots, and stir for 2 to 3 minutes.

4. Add all remaining ingredients and stir well.

5. Reduce heat to medium-low, cover, and cook for about 50 to 60 minutes.

6. Remove from heat; taste and adjust the salt and pepper to taste.

7. Allow to cool down and store in an airtight container; keep refrigerated up to 5 days.

Nutrition Facts

Percent daily values based on the Reference Daily Intake (RDI) for a 2000 calorie diet.

Amount Per Serving

Calories 162.24 | Calories From Fat (15%) 23.79 | Total Fat 2.69g 4% | Saturated Fat 0.58g 3% | Cholesterol 1.38mg <1% | Sodium 982.38mg 41% | Potassium 808.6mg 23% | Total Carbohydrates 30.6g 10% | Fiber 6g 24% | Sugar 9g | Protein 6g 12%

DELICIOUS BREADED TOFU STICKS

Ready in Time: 25 minutes | Servings: 4

Ingredients

1 block extra-firm tofu, well-drained (16 ounces)

4 cloves garlic finely minced

1 Tbsp of mustard

1 Tbsp corn syrup

2 Tbsp tomato paste

1 Tbsp tamari sauce

1 Tbsp water

Salt and ground black pepper to taste

3/4 cup breadcrumbs

1/2 cup of sesame oil for frying

Instructions

1. Drain well the tofu, and cut into strips/pieces/sticks; set aside.

2. Whisk the minced garlic, mustard, corn syrup, tomato paste, tamari sauce, water, and the salt and the pepper in one bowl.

3. In a separate dish/bowl, add the breadcrumbs.

4. Dip the tofu steaks evenly in the garlic mixture.

5. Then, dip your tofu steak into the breadcrumbs.

6. Heat the oil in a frying skillet over medium heat.

7. Fry breaded tofu for about 5 minutes per side; gently flips tofu once.

8. Remove tofu on a plate lined with a paper towel, and allow to drain and cool completely.

9. Store in an airtight container and keep refrigerated up to 3 to 4 days.

Nutrition Facts

Percent daily values based on the Reference Daily Intake (RDI) for a 2000 calorie diet.

Amount Per Serving

Calories 456.33 | Calories From Fat (67%) 307.42 | Total Fat 35.17g 54% | Saturated Fat 4.75g 24% | Cholesterol 0mg 0% | Sodium 524.33mg 22% | Potassium 298.4mg 9% | Total Carbohydrates 24.1g 8% | Fiber 2g 8% | Sugar 4.4g | Protein 15.11g 30%

EGGPLANT AND PARSLEY PUREE

Ready in Time: 20 minutes | Servings: 6

Ingredients

2 lbs eggplants cut into cubes

1 cup fresh parsley leaves

3 cloves garlic, minced

1 green bell pepper, cored and roughly chopped

2 cup of water

1 cup of extra-virgin olive oil

2 Tbsp fresh lemon juice (2 lemons)

Salt and freshly ground black pepper, to taste

Instructions

1. Peel and rinse eggplant; cut eggplant in cubes, and add into Instant pot along with garlic, green pepper, and parsley, and water.

2. Lock lid into place and set on the MANUAL setting high pressure for 5 minutes.

3. When the beep sounds, quick release the pressure by pressing Cancel, and twisting the steam handle to the Venting position.

4. Transfer vegetables into a blender along with oil, lemon juice, and the salt and pepper to taste.

5. Blend until smooth and well combined.

6. Store in an airtight container and keep refrigerated up to 3 to 4 days.

Nutrition Facts

Percent daily values based on the Reference Daily Intake (RDI) for a 2000 calorie diet.

Amount Per Serving

Calories 167.31 | Calories From Fat (95%) 159.3 | Total Fat 18g 28% | Saturated Fat 2.5g 13% | Cholesterol 0mg 0% | Sodium 1.39mg <1% | Potassium 53.6mg 2% | Total Carbohydrates 2g <1% | Fiber 0.46g 2% | Sugar 0.72g | Protein 0.32g <1%

FRESH GARDEN VEGETABLE SOUP

Ready in Time: 20 minutes | Servings: 5

Ingredients

4 Tbsp olive oil

1 onion finely diced

2 cloves garlic finely sliced

Salt and ground black pepper to taste

2 carrots, peeled and sliced

2 celery sticks, sliced

1 cup kale leaves chopped

1 zucchini, diced

1 cup dried mushrooms

1 cup tomatoes peeled and grated

4 cups vegetable broth

1 bay leaf

1 tsp fresh parsley leaves

1 tsp fresh basil leaves

Instructions

1. Turn on the Instant Pot and press the SAUTÉ button.

2. Add olive oil, and sauté onion, and garlic with the pinch of salt for about 2 to 3 minutes.

3. Add sliced carrots and celery, and stir for one minute.

4. Add kale, zucchini, and mushrooms; stir for one minute.

5. Add grated tomatoes, and stir well.

6. Add the vegetable broth along with all remaining ingredients, and stir well.

7. Lock lid into place and set on the MANUAL setting high pressure for 5 minutes.

8. Once the pot beeps finished, use a Quick release.

9. Taste and adjust the salt and pepper to taste.

10. Allow soup to cool completely.

11. Store soup in an airtight container, and refrigerate up to 5 days or freeze up to two months.

Nutrition Facts

Percent daily values based on the Reference Daily Intake (RDI) for a 2000 calorie diet.

Amount Per Serving

Calories 262.92 | Calories From Fat (48%) 126.6 | Total Fat 14.31g 22% | Saturated Fat 2.28g 11% | Cholesterol 1.97mg <1% | Sodium 1329.49mg 55% | Potassium 681.1mg 19% | Total Carbohydrates 28.68g 10% | Fiber 4.64g 19% | Sugar 2.79g | Protein 7g 14%

Fried Tofu with Asparagus and Chinese Sauce

Ready in Time: 25 minutes | Servings: 4

Ingredients

14 oz extra firm tofu

3 Tbsp sesame oil

1 Tbsp soy sauce

1 lb of asparagus cut into 2-inch long pieces

2 Tbsp green onions finely chopped

For the Sauce:

4 Tbsp Tamari sauce (or soy sauce)

4 Tbsp sesame oil

2 Tbsp rice vinegar

4 cloves garlic minced

1 tsp ginger freshly grated

1/4 cup brown sugar

Instructions

1. Cut the block of tofu in half.

2. Gently press tofu halves between paper towels to remove any liquid; cut the tofu into 1/2-inch cubes.

3. Heat oil in a large wok/frying skillet over medium-high heat.

4. Fry tofu cubes until tofu are lightly golden brown

5. Add soy sauce and toss to combine well.

6. Transfer tofu in a bowl, and set aside.

7. In the same wok/frying skillet sauté asparagus and green onions until soft.

8. Transfer vegetables in a bowl with tofu.

53

9. Whisk all sauce ingredients in a bowl until combined well.

10. Pour sauce over vegetables and tofu, and toss to combine well.

11. Taste and adjust seasonings if needed.

12. Store in an airtight container and keep refrigerated up to 4 to 5 days.

Nutrition Facts

Percent daily values based on the Reference Daily Intake (RDI) for a 2000 calorie diet.

Amount Per Serving

Calories 386.14 | Calories From Fat (67%) 259.3 | Total Fat 29.71g 46% | Saturated Fat 4g 20% | Cholesterol 0mg 0% | Sodium 1153.52mg 48% | Potassium 405.92mg 12% | Total Carbohydrates 23.88g 8% | Fiber 2.13g 9% | Sugar 15.58g | Protein 13.6g 27%

FRIED TOMATO SAUCE

Ready in Time: 40 minutes | Servings: 8

Ingredients

4 Tbsp virgin olive oil

1 small onion finely diced

2 cloves chopped garlic

3 lbs of tomatoes, peeled, seeded, and chopped

salt and ground pepper to taste

1/2 cup of ground almonds

1 bay leaf

2 sprigs of parsley

1/2 cup vegetable broth

Instructions

1. Heat oil in a large pot and sauté the onion and garlic with a pinch of salt and pepper until soft.

2. Add tomatoes and cook, often stirring on high heat for 2 to 3 minutes.

3. Add all remaining ingredients and bring to boil.

4. Reduce heat to medium-low, cover, and cook for 15 - 20 minutes.

5. Transfer mixture to a blender; blend the mixture with an immersion blender until soft.

6. Allow the sauce to cool completely, store in a container, and keep refrigerated up to a week.

7. Also, you can freeze your sauce in a freezer bag for up to 3 months

Nutrition Facts

Percent daily values based on the Reference Daily Intake (RDI) for a 2000 calorie diet.

Amount Per Serving

Calories 161 | Calories From Fat (62%) 100.33 | Total Fat 11.6g 18% | Saturated Fat 1.34g 7% | Cholesterol 0mg 0% | Sodium 46.86mg 2% | Potassium 501.7mg 14% | Total Carbohydrates 10.53g 4% | Fiber 3.27g 13% | Sugar 5.7g | Protein 3.55g 7%

HEARTY AND CREAMY CORN CHOWDER

Ready in Time: 20 minutes | Servings: 4

Ingredients

2 cups of frozen whole kernel corn

2 Tbsp chopped onion

1 tsp of grated garlic

2 Tbsp finely chopped parsley

4 Tbsp chopped green pepper

1 1/2 cups of vegetable broth

2 Tbsp olive oil

Salt and ground pepper to taste

1 cup of almond milk

2 Tbsp yellow cornmeal

Instructions

1. Add corn, onion, garlic, parsley, green pepper, salt and pepper, vegetable broth, and olive oil in your Instant Pot; stir.

2. Dissolve cornmeal in almond milk and pour in Instant pot; give a good stir.

3. Lock lid into place and set on the MANUAL setting high pressure for 10 minutes.

4. When the timer beeps, press "Cancel" and carefully flip the Quick Release valve to let the pressure out.

5. Taste and adjust the salt and pepper to taste; allow to cool completely.

6. Store your chowder in an airtight container, and keep refrigerated up to 4 days.

Note: *For quick and easy reheating, store single-serving portions in individual containers.*

Nutrition Facts

Percent daily values based on the Reference Daily Intake (RDI) for a 2000 calorie diet.

Amount Per Serving

Calories 225.14 | Calories From Fat (39%) 86.92 | Total Fat 9.67g 15% | Saturated Fat 1.2g 6% | Cholesterol 0mg 0% | Sodium 448mg 19% | Potassium 456.18mg 13% | Total Carbohydrates 32.58g 11% | Fiber 4g 16% | Sugar 4.6g | Protein 6.7g 14%

HIGH-PROTEIN QUINOA WITH CELERY AND PINE NUTS

Ready in Time: 25 minutes | Servings: 4

Ingredients

4 Tbsp olive oil

2 green onions sliced

1 cup quinoa

1/4 cup pine nuts

4 stalks celery, chopped

3 cups vegetable broth

Sea salt to taste

1/4 cup fresh lemon juice

1/4 tsp cayenne pepper

1/2 tsp ground cumin

2 Tbsp fresh parsley chopped

Instructions

1. Turn on the Instant Pot and press the SAUTÉ button and heat oil.

2. Sauté the green onion with a pinch of salt until soft.

3. Add quinoa and peanuts, and stir for one minute.

4. Add celery, and all remaining ingredients and give a good stir.

5. Lock lid into place and set on the MANUAL setting high pressure for 3 minutes.

6. Once the pot beeps finished, use a natural release for 10 minutes.

7. Remove from the pot and allow to cool down.

8. Store in an airtight container in a fridge for up to 5 days.

Nutrition Facts

Percent daily values based on the Reference Daily Intake (RDI) for a 2000 calorie diet.

Amount Per Serving

Calories 470.37 | Calories From Fat (46%) 218.64 | Total Fat 24.6g 38% | Saturated Fat 3.28g 16% | Cholesterol 1.85mg <1% | Sodium 1602.8mg 67% | Potassium 751.2mg 21% | Total Carbohydrates 51.52g 17% | Fiber 6.79g 27% | Sugar 1.73g | Protein 12.56g 25%

INSTANT FAVA BEAN SOUP WITH SAFFRON

Ready in Time: 40 minutes | Servings: 4

Ingredients

4 Tbsp olive oil

1 yellow onion finely diced

2 cloves garlic, chopped

Kosher salt and freshly ground black pepper, to taste

1 1/2 cups Fava Bean (broad beans)

1 can (11 oz) tomatoes - diced

4 cups vegetable broth

1 tsp crushed saffron threads (or 1/2 tsp of ground turmeric)

1 tsp ground cumin

Instructions

1. Turn on the Instant Pot and press the SAUTÉ button; heat oil.

2. Sauté onion and garlic with the pinch of salt, often stirring, for about 2 to 3 minutes.

3. Add fava beans and tomatoes; stir for one minute.

4. Add the vegetable broth, and all remaining ingredients, and stir well.

5. Lock lid into place and set on the MANUAL setting high pressure for 30 minutes.

6. Use Quick Release - turn the valve from sealing to venting to release the pressure.

7. Allow it to cool completely.

8. Store in an airtight container and keep refrigerated up to 4 to 5 days.

9. You can also freeze your fava beans soup in freezer bags for up to six months.

Nutrition Facts

Percent daily values based on the Reference Daily Intake (RDI) for a 2000 calorie diet.

Amount Per Serving

Calories 331.33 | Calories From Fat (46%) 153.58 | Total Fat 17.37g 27% | Saturated Fat 2.72g 14% | Cholesterol 2.15mg <1% | Sodium 1548.13mg 65% | Potassium 695.25mg 20% | Total Carbohydrates 37.2g 13% | Fiber 4.14g 17% | Sugar 3.17g | Protein 10g 20%

INSTANT LENTILS BOLOGNESE

Ready in Time: 35 minutes | Servings: 5

Ingredients

4 Tbsp olive oil

1 large onion

2 cloves garlic finely chopped

Salt and ground pepper to taste

2 cup of red lentils

1 carrot sliced

1 can (15 oz) peeled tomatoes

4 cups of vegetable broth

1 Tbsp Italian seasoning

Instructions

1. Press the SAUTÉ button on your Instant Pot, and add oil.

2. Sauté the onion and garlic with a pinch of salt until soft or for about 3 minutes.

3. Add lentils and stir for a further one minute.

4. Add carrots and tomatoes, and stir for one minute.

5. Add broth and Italian seasoning.

6. Lock lid into place and set on the MANUAL setting high pressure for 15 minutes.

7. Once cooking completes, let the pressure valve release naturally (about 10 minutes), and quick-release remaining pressure.

8. Taste and adjust seasonings; allow it to cool completely.

9. Store in a covered glass or airtight container in the fridge for up to 4 days.

10. Or, you can freeze your lentils for two months.

Nutrition Facts

Percent daily values based on the Reference Daily Intake (RDI) for a 2000 calorie diet.

Amount Per Serving

Calories 522.2 | Calories From Fat (25%) 131.53 | Total Fat 14.85g 23% | Saturated Fat 2.34g 12% | Cholesterol 2mg <1% | Sodium 1372.65mg 57% | Potassium 1206.23mg 34% | Total Carbohydrates 73.36g 24% | Fiber 27.37g 109% | Sugar 4.28g | Protein 25.42g 51%

Jasmine Rice and Peas Risotto

Ready in Time: 25 minutes | Servings: 4

Ingredients

4 Tbsp olive oil

1 medium onion finely diced

2 cloves garlic minced

Salt and ground black pepper to taste

1 1/2 cups dry jasmine rice (or long grain rice)

1/2 cup of green peas

1 bay leaf

2 cups of vegetable broth

2 cups of water

Instructions

1. Press the SAUTÉ button on your Instant Pot.

2. When the word "hot" appears on display, add the oil and sauté the onion and garlic with a pinch of salt for about 5 minutes; stir frequently.

3. Add the jasmine rice and stir for one minute.

4. Add green peas, and all remaining ingredients and stir well.

5. Lock lid into place and set on the RICE setting high pressure for 6 minutes.

6. When the timer beeps, press "Cancel" and use a Natural release for 10 to 15 minutes.

7. Taste and adjust the salt and pepper to taste.

8. Allow cooling completely.

9. Store your risotto in an airtight container, and keep refrigerated up to 4 to 5 days.

Nutrition Facts

Percent daily values based on the Reference Daily Intake (RDI) for a 2000 calorie diet.

Amount Per Serving

Calories 421 | Calories From Fat (34%) 144.5 | Total Fat 16.58g 26% | Saturated Fat 2.1g 11% | Cholesterol 0mg 0% | Sodium 59.4mg 2% | Potassium 181mg 5% | Total Carbohydrates 67.1g 22% | Fiber 5.81g 23% | Sugar 2.3g | Protein 8.21g 16%

SIMPLE LENTIL SOUP

Ready in Time: 35 minutes | Servings: 6

Ingredients

4 Tbsp olive oil

1 medium onion, chopped

2 cloves garlic minced

3/4 tsp   kosher salt and fresh ground black pepper

1 1/2 cups mature seeds lentils

2 large carrots sliced

1 medium potato, peeled and diced

1 cup tomato juice

4 cups vegetable broth

2 bay leaves

2 Tbsp fresh thyme finely chopped

Instructions

1. Turn on the Instant Pot and press the SAUTÉ button.

2. When the word "hot" appears on display, add the oil and sauté the onions and garlic with a pinch of salt and pepper for about 2 to 3 minutes.

3. Add lentils, carrot, and potato and stir for one minute.

4. Pour the tomato juice, broth, and all remaining ingredients; stir for one minute.

5. Lock lid into place and set on the MANUAL setting high pressure for 15 minutes.

6. Release pressure naturally for 10 minutes and quick-release remaining pressure.

7. Taste and adjust seasonings to taste; allow soup to cool completely.

8. Store soup in an airtight container and refrigerate for up to 3 days.

9. Or, pour soup into freezer bags, and freeze for one month.

Nutrition Facts

Percent daily values based on the Reference Daily Intake (RDI) for a 2000 calorie diet.

Amount Per Serving

Calories 409.1 | Calories From Fat (26%) 108.2 | Total Fat 12.21g 19% | Saturated Fat 2g 10% | Cholesterol 1.64mg <1% | Sodium 1347.3mg 56% | Potassium 1061.31mg 30% | Total Carbohydrates 58.44g 19% | Fiber 18.81g 75% | Sugar 4.81g | Protein 17.85g 36%

OVEN-BAKED PEAS FRITTERS

Ready in Time: 35 minutes | Servings: 4

Ingredients

4 Tbsp olive oil

1 onion, finely diced

2 garlic cloves, minced

A pinch of salt and ground black pepper

2 cups boiled peas, drained

1 1/2 cups chickpea flour

1 tsp baking soda

1/2 tsp turmeric

2 Tbsp Italian seasonings

Instructions

1. Preheat your oven 350F.

2. Line a baking tray with baking paper; set aside.

3. Heat oil in a frying skillet, and sauté the onion with a pinch of salt until softened.

4. Add drained peas, and stir for a further two minutes.

5. Add the mixture to a food processor and pulse until combined well.

6. Stir in the chickpea flour, soda, turmeric, salt, pepper, and Italian seasoning.

7. Shape the mixture into round balls/patties; arrange balls/patties onto a prepared baking tray.

8. Bake for 16 to18 minutes or until golden brown.

9. Remove from the oven, and allow fritters to cool completely.

10. Store your fritters in an airtight container and keep refrigerated for up to 3 days or freeze them up to a month.

11. To reheat frozen fritters, place them on a baking paper-lined sheet and heat on a 400 F oven for 15 minutes.

Nutrition Facts

Percent daily values based on the Reference Daily Intake (RDI) for a 2000 calorie diet.

Amount Per Serving

Calories 415.14 | Calories From Fat (36%) 151 | Total Fat 17.28g 27% | Saturated Fat 2.28g 11% | Cholesterol 0mg 0% | Sodium 703.8mg 29% | Potassium 557.92mg 16% | Total Carbohydrates 51.44g 17% | Fiber 9.66g 39% | Sugar 5.45g | Protein 14.2g 28%

Robust Potato, Rice, and Spinach Soup

Ready in Time: 25 minutes | Servings: 6

Ingredients

4 Tbsp olive oil

4 sliced leeks

3 crushed garlic cloves

1 tsp salt and ground black pepper to taste

1 cup rice long grained

3 potatoes (cut in large chunks)

4 cups vegetable broth

1 cup fresh spinach

1/4 cup fresh parsley finely chopped

1/4 cup fresh celery finely chopped

2 Tbsp fresh lemon juice

2 Tbsp tomato paste

1 bay leaf

2 tsp dried basil

Instructions

1. Turn on the Instant Pot and press the SAUTÉ button; heat oil.

2. Sauté leeks and garlic with the pinch of salt, occasionally stirring, for about 3 to 4 minutes.

3. Add rice and potato, and stir for about 2 minutes.

4. Add spinach and all remaining ingredients and stir well.

5. Lock lid into place and set on the MANUAL setting high pressure for 8 minutes.

6. Allow the pressure to release naturally for 10 minutes and then release any remaining pressure.

7. Once all of the pressure releases, the steam will no longer come out of the vent, and you'll be able to open the lid.

8. Taste and adjust the salt and pepper.

9. Refrigerate cooked soup in an airtight container up to 5 days.

10. Or, freeze in heavy-duty freezer bags for up to one month.

Nutrition Facts

Percent daily values based on the Reference Daily Intake (RDI) for a 2000 calorie diet.

Amount Per Serving

Calories 365.17 | Calories From Fat (29%) 106.3 | Total Fat 12g 18% | Saturated Fat 1.93g 10% | Cholesterol 1.64mg <1% | Sodium 1542.4mg 64% | Potassium 899mg 26% | Total Carbohydrates 57.51g 19% | Fiber 5.94g 24% | Sugar 3.8g | Protein 8.5g 17%

Spiced Cabbage, Soybeans and Peanuts Stew

Ready in Time: 15 minutes | Servings: 4

Instructions

3 cups cabbage, finely chopped

3/4 cup of soybeans in the pod

2 large carrots sliced

1 small red pepper, diced

1 Tbsp minced garlic

1/2 cup of peanuts

1/4 cup of olive oil

salt and pepper, to taste

1/4 cup of soy sauce

1/2 cup of water

1 lime freshly juiced

1/4 tsp of garlic powder

1/4 tsp of ginger powder

Instructions

1. Add all ingredients in an 8-quart Instant Pot.

2. Stir to combine well.

3. Lock lid into place and set on the MANUAL setting for 8 minutes.

4. When the beep sounds, quick release the pressure by pressing Cancel, and twisting the steam handle to the Venting position.

5. Once all of the pressure releases, the steam will no longer come out of the vent, and you'll be able to open the lid.

6. Taste and adjust seasonings; leave it to cool completely.

7. Keep refrigerated in an airtight container up to 3 days or freeze in freezer bags up to 2 months.

Nutrition Facts

Percent daily values based on the Reference Daily Intake (RDI) for a 2000 calorie diet.

Amount Per Serving

Calories 351 | Calories From Fat (58%) 203.43 | Total Fat 23.4g 36% | Saturated Fat 3.24g 16% | Cholesterol 0mg 0% | Sodium 744.31mg 31% | Potassium 535.31mg 15% | Total Carbohydrates 29.46g 10% | Fiber 7.5g 30% | Sugar 5.74g | Protein 9.7g 19%

Vegan Potato and Mushroom Frittata

Ready in Time: 40 minutes | Servings: 4

Ingredients

1 lb waxy potatoes, cut into medium slices

1 large onion finely sliced

1 cup chickpea flour

1 cup dried mushrooms sliced

2 Tbsp fresh parsley finely chopped

Salt and ground black pepper to taste

4 Tbsp olive oil

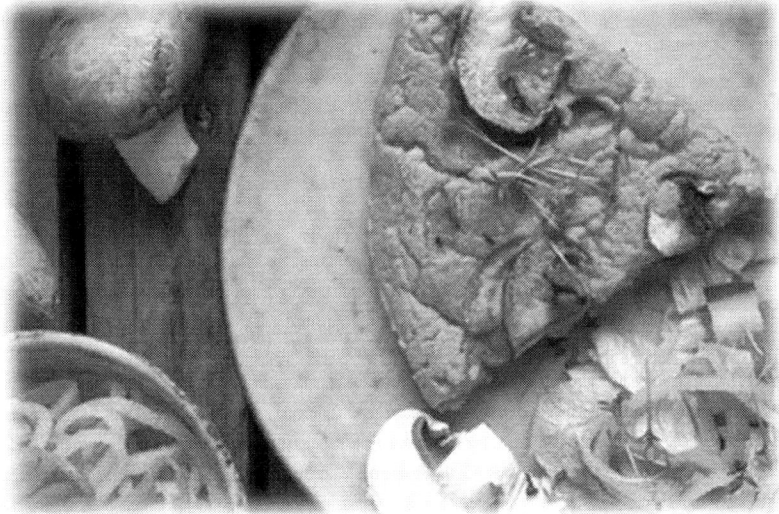

Instructions

1. Cook potatoes in gently boiling water until tender or for about 18 to 20 minutes.

2. Drain in a colander and allow to cool a bit.

3. Place potatoes in a large bowl and add onion, chickpeas, mushrooms, parsley, and salt and pepper.

4. Mash with the fork, and then knead the mixture with your hand until combined well.

5. Heat oil into large frying skillet and add the potato mixture; cook for about 6 to 8 minutes over medium heat.

6. Gently flip it over, and cook from the other side for about 3 minutes.

7. Remove from skillet and place on a plate to cool down.

8. Cut into slices and store in an airtight container; keep refrigerated up to 3 to 4 days.

Nutrition Facts

Percent daily values based on the Reference Daily Intake (RDI) for a 2000 calorie diet.

Amount Per Serving

Calories 226 | Calories From Fat (59%) 133.24 | Total Fat 15.16g 23% | Saturated Fat 2.05g 10% | Cholesterol 0mg 0% | Sodium 19.21mg <1% | Potassium 328.12mg 9% | Total Carbohydrates 17.11g 6% | Fiber 3.35g 13% | Sugar 4.35g | Protein 6g 12%

DINNER

ARTICHOKE HEARTHS WITH BROWN RICE

Preparation Time: 40 minutes | Servings: 4

Ingredients

1 cup of avocado oil (or sesame oil)

10 canned artichoke hearts, drained and chopped

1 cup cauliflower (divided into florets)

1 cup of brown rice

3 cups of vegetable broth

2 Tbsp of fresh parsley finely chopped

2 Tbsp fresh dill finely chopped

2 Tbsp lemon juice freshly squeezed

salt and ground pepper to taste

Instructions

1. Heat oil in a large pot over medium-high heat.

2. Add artichoke hearts and sauté for 5 minutes.

3. Add the cauliflower and sprinkle with the pinch of the salt and pepper; stir for two minutes.

4. Add all remaining ingredients and give a good stir.

5. Bring to a boil and reduce heat to medium.

6. Cover and cook for 25 minutes.

7. Taste and adjust seasonings.

8. Allow to cool down completely.

9. Store in a large airtight container and keep refrigerated up to 4 to 5 days.

10. To reheat, place the rice and artichokes into a heatproof dish and add little water or broth; cover and microwave on HIGH for approximately 1 to 2 minutes.

Nutrition Facts

Percent daily values based on the Reference Daily Intake (RDI) for a 2000 calorie diet.

Amount Per Serving

Calories 581.35 | Calories From Fat (45%) 263.17 | Total Fat 29.81g 46% | Saturated Fat 3.69g 18% | Cholesterol 1.23mg <1% | Sodium 1056mg 44% | Potassium 932.39mg 27% | Total Carbohydrates 72.6g 24% | Fiber 11.35g 45% | Sugar 0.69g | Protein 12.69g 25%

BAKED SWEET POTATO WITH GREEN BEANS

Ready in Time: 1 hour and 10 minutes | Servings: 5

Ingredients

2 lbs sweet potatoes cut into cubes

1 tsp pumpkin pie spice

1/3 cup olive oil

3/4 lb canned green beans, drained

1 cup mushrooms (chopped fine)

1 1/2 cups of water

Salt and ground black pepper to taste

Instructions

1. Preheat oven to 350 F.

2. Grease 9-inch baking dish; set aside.

3. Blend the sweet potato cubes, oil, and pumpkin pie spice in a large bowl.

4. Cover and let it sit for about 5 minutes or until smooth.

5. Arrange the sweet potato mixture over the prepared baking dish, and cover with the green beans mixture.

6. Bake for about 1 hour or until sweet potato is soft.

7. Adjust seasonings and allow to cool completely.

8. Store in an airtight container and keep refrigerated up to 4 days.

Nutrition Facts

Percent daily values based on the Reference Daily Intake (RDI) for a 2000 calorie diet.

Amount Per Serving

Calories 158.78 | Calories From Fat (82%) 129.44 | Total Fat 14.65g 23% | Saturated Fat 2g 10% | Cholesterol 0mg 0% | Sodium 6.19mg <1% | Potassium 192.27mg 5% | Total Carbohydrates 6g 2% | Fiber 2.04g 8% | Sugar 2g | Protein 1.64g 3%

BEANS AND CAULIFLOWER SOUP

Ready in Time: 25 minutes | Servings: 6

Ingredients

1/4 cup olive oil

1 large onion cut in chunks

2 cloves garlic finely chopped

salt and ground pepper, to taste

2 can (11 oz) white beans

2 cups cauliflower

2 Tbsp chopped parsley

3 sprigs thyme

pepper

3 1/2 cups vegetable broth

Instructions

1. Heat oil in a large pot over medium-high heat.

2. Sauté the onion and garlic with a pinch of salt until soft and translucent.

3. Add white beans and stir for two minutes.

4. Add cauliflower and stir for one minute.

5. Add all remaining ingredients and stir for one minute.

6. Reduce heat to medium, cover, and cook for 10 minutes.

7. Remove the bean soup in a blender; blend until smooth.

8. Store in an airtight container in the fridge up to 5 days or freeze up to two months.

Nutrition Facts

Percent daily values based on the Reference Daily Intake (RDI) for a 2000 calorie diet.

Amount Per Serving

Calories 463.8 | Calories From Fat (23%) 107.56 | Total Fat 12.19g 19% | Saturated Fat 2g 10% | Cholesterol 2.88mg <1% | Sodium 637.61mg 27% | Potassium 1941mg 55% | Total Carbohydrates 66.48g 22% | Fiber 15.16g 61% | Sugar 3.47g | Protein 25.43g 51%

Beans, Sesame and Pine Nuts Puree

Ready in Time: 20 minutes | Servings: 4

Ingredients

1 lb broad beans

2 cups boiling water

salt and ground black pepper to taste

1/3 cup sesame or avocado oil

1 tsp garlic powder

1/4 cup roasted pine nuts

1 Tbsp sesame seeds

1 Tbsp lemon juice, freshly squeezed

Instructions

1. Boil beans in a large pot for 2 minutes, throw water, and rinse them.

2. Add fresh water, a little salt, and boil broad beans for about 7 to 8 minutes.

3. Transfer broad beans into a high-speed blender along with all remaining ingredients blend until soft.

4. Taste and adjust seasonings.

5. Store in an airtight container and ref up to 5 days.

Nutrition Facts

Percent daily values based on the Reference Daily Intake (RDI) for a 2000 calorie diet.

Amount Per Serving

Calories 323.6 | Calories From Fat (66%) 214.7 | Total Fat 24.64g 38% | Saturated Fat 3.04g 15% | Cholesterol 0mg 0% | Sodium 106.16mg 4% | Potassium 458.62mg 13% | Total Carbohydrates 23.15g 8% | Fiber 0.52g 2% | Sugar 0.73g | Protein 10.38g 21%

BELUGA LENTILS AND TOFU 'MEATBALLS'

Ready in Time: 1 hour and 25 minutes | Servings: 3

Ingredients

1 cup black lentils uncooked

1 tsp fennel seed

1 cup quinoa (uncooked

Kosher salt and ground black pepper to taste

1 tsp granulated garlic

1/4 cup fresh cilantro finely chopped

6 oz extra- firm tofu, pressed down, patted dry and cut into tiny cubes

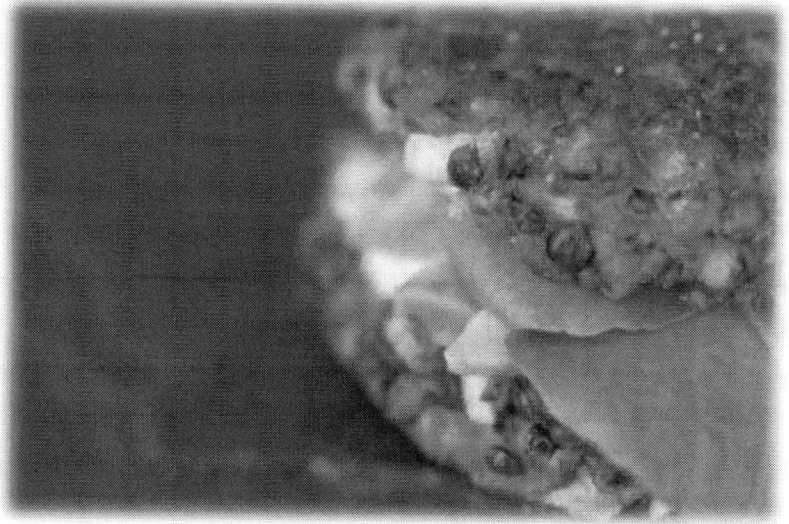

2 Tbs olive oil

Instructions

1. Heat water (about 3 cups) over high heat and add lentils, fennel, and a pinch of salt and pepper.

2. Bring lentils to a boil, and turn heat medium-low.

3. Cover and cook for about 25 minutes.

4. When ready, rinse, and drain well.

5. In a small pot, add one cup of water and bring quinoa to boil.

6. Cover and simmer for 15 minutes; rinse and drain.

7. Preheat oven to 400 F.

8. Line a baking sheet with parchment paper; set aside.

9. Combine lentils and quinoa in a food processor.

10. Add all remaining ingredients, season generously with the salt and pepper; pulse until the texture of coarse sand.

11. Shape the mixture into 'meat' balls.

12. Place lentil balls onto a prepared baking sheet, and bake for 20 to 25 minutes.

13. Remove from the oven, and allow to cool completely.

14. Store in an airtight container in the fridge for up to 5 days.

15. Or, pack 'meatballs' in freezer bags and keep in freezer up to 3 months.

Nutrition Facts

Percent daily values based on the Reference Daily Intake (RDI) for a 2000 calorie diet.

Amount Per Serving

Calories 468.29 | Calories From Fat (28%) 129.82 | Total Fat 14.84g 23% | Saturated Fat 1.86g 9% | Cholesterol 0mg 0% | Sodium 13.4mg <1% | Potassium 895.34mg 26% | Total Carbohydrates 59g 20% | Fiber 22.23g 89% | Sugar 1.61g | Protein 26.5g 53%

BLACK EYED BEANS WITH SPINACH

Ready in Time: 40 minutes | Servings: 6

Ingredients

1/2 lb black-eyed peas

1/2 cup olive oil

1 carrot, sliced 1" thick

2 green onions (only white parts)

2 stalks of celery

1 lb fresh spinach roughly chopped

1 lemon, juiced

1 tsp garlic powder

salt and black pepper, freshly ground

1/2 cup tomato juice

1 cup vegetable broth

Instructions

1. Rinse the beans and place them in your Instant Pot.

2. Add all remaining ingredients and stir well.

3. Lock lid into place and set on the MANUAL setting high pressure for 25 minutes.

4. Release pressure naturally for 10 minutes and quick-release remaining pressure.

5. Taste and adjust seasonings to taste.

6. Serve hot.

7. Allow cooling completely.

8. Keep refrigerated in an airtight container up to 4 to 5 days.

Nutrition Facts

Percent daily values based on the Reference Daily Intake (RDI) for a 2000 calorie diet.

Amount Per Serving

Calories 363 | Calories From Fat (47%) 172.1 | Total Fat 19.51g 30% | Saturated Fat 2.77g 14% | Cholesterol 0.41mg <1% | Sodium 361.9mg 15% | Potassium 1057.24mg 30% | Total Carbohydrates 37.19g 12% | Fiber 13.26g 53% | Sugar 6.6g | Protein 13.33g 27%

EGGPLANTS WITH PEPPERCORN - TAMARI SAUCE

Ready in Time: 35 minutes | Servings: 6

Ingredients

1 1/2 lbs eggplants cut into 4 x 10-inch pieces

pinch of salt

1/3 cup peanut oil

4 cloves garlic chopped

2 tsp fresh ginger, finely minced

5 to 6 dried red chilies

1/2 cup of lukewarm water

Peppercorn - Tamari Sauce

1 tsp peppercorns

1/3 cup of tamari sauce

1 tsp chili flakes

2 Tbsp sesame oil

1 Tbsp vinegar (any)

2 Tbsp of dark honey

1/4 tsp of cinnamon

Instructions

1. Peal, clean, and sprinkle eggplant pieces with the salt, and brush with the oil.

2. Heat the peanut oil in a wok or large frying skillet over medium-high heat.

3. Sauté garlic with the pinch of salt for about 3 to 4 minutes.

4. Add eggplants, ginger, and red chilies, and stir for two minutes.

5. Pour water, reduce heat to medium-low, cover, and cook for 10 minutes.

6. In the meantime, prepare the sauce; combine all sauce ingredients in a bowl.

7. Pour sauce into wok/frying skillet, stir, and cook for a further 2 to 3 minutes.

8. Remove from the heat, and allow it to cool completely.

9. Store in an airtight container in the fridge for up to 4 to 5 days.

Nutrition Facts

Percent daily values based on the Reference Daily Intake (RDI) for a 2000 calorie diet.

Amount Per Serving

Calories 252.6 | Calories From Fat (60%) 150.5 | Total Fat 17.06g 26% | Saturated Fat 2.76g 14% | Cholesterol 0mg 0% | Sodium 1152.58mg 53% | Potassium 614.58mg 18% | Total Carbohydrates 24.65g 8% | Fiber 4.36g 17% | Sugar 9.15g | Protein 5g 10%

Garlic Black Beans and Rice Stew

Ready in Time: 40 minutes | Servings: 5

Ingredients

4 Tbsp of sesame oil

6 cloves minced garlic

Salt and Freshly-ground black pepper to taste

2 cups long-grain rice

1 can of black beans drained

4 cups vegetable broth

1/2 cup of soy sauce

1/2 cup of tomato sauce or crushed tomatoes

Instructions

1. Heat oil in a large skillet over medium-high heat; saute the garlic with a pinch of salt and pepper, constantly stirring, for about 3 to 4 minutes.

2. Add the black beans and rice, and stir for further two minutes.

3. Add the broth, soy sauce, and tomato sauce; stir for one minute.

4. Bring to a boil, reduce heat to medium, cover, and cook for 20 to 25 minutes.

5. Remove from the heat, and adjust the salt and pepper.

6. Store in an airtight container and keep refrigerated up to 4 to 5 days.

Nutrition Facts

Percent daily values based on the Reference Daily Intake (RDI) for a 2000 calorie diet.

Amount Per Serving

Calories 486 | Calories From Fat (27%) 130.35 | Total Fat 14.6g 23% | Saturated Fat 2.41g 12% | Cholesterol 1.7mg <1% | Sodium 1446.61mg 62% | Potassium 704.91mg 20% | Total Carbohydrates 73.3g 24% | Fiber 9.91g 40% | Sugar 1.53g | Protein 15.7g 31%

GIGANTE BEANS AND TOMATOES STEW

Ready in Time: 1 hour and 10 minutes | Servings: 6

Ingredients

3/4 lbs Gigante Beans soaked overnight

1/2 cup of olive oil

1 large onion, finely chopped

3 cloves garlic finely sliced

salt and freshly ground pepper

3/4 lb grated tomatoes or canned peeled tomatoes

1/2 bunch of parsley, finely chopped

1/2 Tbsp fresh thyme

1/2 tsp crushed red pepper flakes

2 cups of vegetable broth

2 cups of water

Instructions

1. Soak the Gigante beans covered in a warm place.

2. Press the SAUTÉ button on your Instant Pot and heat the oil.

3. Sauté the onion and garlic with a pinch of salt and pepper until soft.

4. Add grated tomatoes and soaked beans; stir for two minutes.

5. Add parsley, thyme, and red flakes; stir.

6. Add water and broth, and give a good stir.

7. Lock lid into place and set on the MANUAL setting high pressure for 50 minutes.

8. Once the pot beeps finished, use the Naturally release for 10 minutes and quick-release remaining pressure.

9. Taste and adjust the salt and pepper to taste.

10. Store in an airtight container, and keep refrigerated up to 4 to 5 days or keep frozen in a freezer-bags up to 4 to 5 months.

Nutrition Facts

Percent daily values based on the Reference Daily Intake (RDI) for a 2000 calorie diet.

Amount Per Serving

Calories 428,43 | Calories From Fat (41%) 175,92 | Total Fat 19.92g 31% | Saturated Fat 2.93g 15% | Cholesterol 0.82mg <1% | Sodium 558.12mg 23% | Potassium 1349.68mg 39% | Total Carbohydrates 48.61g 16% | Fiber 11g 44% | Sugar 3.61g | Protein 16.53g 34%

GREEK RATATOUILLE

Ready in Time: 25 minutes | Servings: 4

Ingredients

3/4 of olive oil

1 onion finely diced

2 cloves garlic finely sliced

Salt and ground pepper to taste

2 potatoes cut into cubes

1 eggplant cut into cubes

1 lb zucchini cut into rings

1 pepper (red-green) sliced

2 Tbs fresh chopped mint, basil, and parsley

1 can (11 oz) of crushed tomatoes

1 tsp tomato paste

1 cup of water

1 vegetable bouillon cube of 1 cup of vegetable broth

Instructions

1. Pour oil to the inner stainless steel pot in the Instant Pot.

2. Turn on the Instant Pot and press the SAUTÉ button.

3. When the word "HOT" appears on display, sauté the onion and garlic with a pinch of the salt and pepper for about 3 to 4 minutes.

4. Add potato and eggplant cubes and stir for one minute.

5. Add zucchini and pepper and stir for one minute.

6. Add fresh chopped mint, basil and parsley, and stir well.

7. Add crushed tomatoes, tomato paste, water, and vegetable bouillon cube or one cup of vegetable broth; stir well.

8. Lock lid into place and set on the MANUAL setting high pressure for 12 minutes.

9. Use Quick Release - turn the valve from sealing to venting to release the pressure.

10. Stir, taste and adjust the salt and pepper to taste.

11. Store in an airtight container in the fridge for up to 4 days.

Nutrition Facts

Percent daily values based on the Reference Daily Intake (RDI) for a 2000 calorie diet.

Amount Per Serving

Calories 184.64 | Calories From Fat (35%) 65.1 | Total Fat 7.39g 11% | Saturated Fat 1.1g 5% | Cholesterol 0mg 0% | Sodium 190.2mg 8% | Potassium 961.61mg 27% | Total Carbohydrates 27.4g 9% | Fiber 4.9g 20% | Sugar 7.73g | Protein 4.61g 9%

Mediterranean Pie Stuffed with Black Olives

Ready in Time: 1 hour and 5 minutes | Servings: 10

Ingredients

For dough

3 1/2 cup of flour all-purposes

2 1 tsp baking soda

1 1/3 cups of olive oil

1 1/4 cups of orange juice

For stuffing

4 Tbsp of olive oil

2 large onions, finely chopped

3 cups of black olives pitted

3 tsp of fresh mint finely chopped

1 tsp sesame seeds toasted

1 tsp cumin seeds, crushed

Instructions

1. Preheat oven to 360 F.

2. Prepare and grease a round baking pan.

3. Combine the flour with the baking powder in a large bowl.

4. Whisk the olive oil and orange juice into a large bowl; stir well.

5. Combine the flour with the oil mixture, and knead well until get a smooth and light dough.

6. Divide dough into 2 sheets.

7. Heat the oil in a frying skillet and sauté onion until translucent; add olives and fresh chopped mint.

8. Stir and cook for about 3 minutes.

9. Place one sheet of dough into a prepared baking dish and spread the filling; sprinkle with sesame seeds and cumin.

10. Cover the mixture with the second sheet and gently chop the pie into pieces.

11. Bake for 45 minutes or until golden brown.

12. Remove from the oven, and let it sit until cool down completely.

13. Store in an airtight container and keep refrigerated up to 4 to 5 days or freeze your pie for up to one month.

Nutrition Facts

Percent daily values based on the Reference Daily Intake (RDI) for a 2000 calorie diet.

Amount Per Serving

Calories 426.55 | Calories From Fat (55%) 232.85 | Total Fat 26.53g 41% | Saturated Fat 3.64g 18% | Cholesterol 0mg 0% | Sodium 475.5mg 20% | Potassium 169.7mg 5% | Total Carbohydrates 42.64g 14% | Fiber 3.14g 13% | Sugar 4.28g | Protein 5.43g 11%

PENNE WITH LEMONY ASPARAGUS

Ready in Time: 30 minutes | Servings: 2

Ingredients

8 oz pasta (of your preference)

2 cups sliced asparagus

4 Tbs olive oil

1/2 cup green onions, chopped

2 cloves garlic minced

2 Tbsp fresh lemon juice

2 tsp lemon rind

salt and ground black pepper to taste

Instructions

1. Cook pasta according to package directions.

2. Add asparagus to pasta during the last 3 minutes of cooking time; drain.

3. Heat oil in a large frying skillet over medium-high heat.

4. Sauté green onions and garlic with a pinch of salt for about 4 to 5 minutes.

5. Add pasta, asparagus, lemon juice, lemon rind, and the salt and pepper to taste.

6. Stir and cook for two minutes.

7. Taste and adjust the salt.

8. Store pasta in an airtight container in the fridge for up to 4 days.

Nutrition Facts

Percent daily values based on the Reference Daily Intake (RDI) for a 2000 calorie diet.

Amount Per Serving

Calories 703.14 | Calories From Fat (37%) 257.34 | Total Fat 29g 45% | Saturated Fat 4.05g 20% | Cholesterol 0mg 0% | Sodium 161.21mg 7% | Potassium 556.6mg 16% | Total Carbohydrates 94.12g 31% | Fiber 6.31g 25% | Sugar 3.64g | Protein 18.16g 36%

Quinoa with Vegetables Briam

Ready in Time: 35 minutes | Servings: 5

Ingredients

4 Tbs olive oil

1 onion finely sliced

2 cloves garlic finely sliced

1 green pepper, chopped

1 red bell pepper

Salt and ground pepper to taste

1 eggplant cut into slices

2 medium zucchini sliced

2 ripped tomatoes grated

1/2 cup quinoa

1 cup of vegetable broth

Instructions

1. Rinse quinoa in a fine-mesh sieve until water runs clear; set aside.

2. Heat oil n a non-stick frying skillet over medium-high heat.

3. Sauté the onion, garlic, peppers, eggplant, and zucchini with a pinch of salt and pepper.

4. Add grated tomato, stir well, cover, and simmer vegetables over medium heat for about 10 minutes.

5. Add quinoa and vegetable broth, stir well, and cook for further 10 to12 minutes or until any liquid is absorbed

6. Remove from the heat, taste, and adjust the salt and pepper to taste.

7. Store in an airtight container in the fridge for up to 4 to 5 days.

8. Or, transfer the quinoa mixture to a resealable freezer bag and keep in freezer up to 6 months.

Nutrition Facts

Percent daily values based on the Reference Daily Intake (RDI) for a 2000 calorie diet.

Amount Per Serving

Calories 262.62 | Calories From Fat (45%) 117.6 | Total Fat 13.31g 20% | Saturated Fat 1.94g 10% | Cholesterol 0.49mg <1% | Sodium 340.63mg 14% | Potassium 879.8mg 25% | Total Carbohydrates 31.84g 11% | Fiber 7.6g 32% | Sugar 8.6g | Protein 6.87g 14%

Roasted Brussels sprouts with Tofu

Ready in Time: 45 minutes | Servings: 4

Ingredients

1 1/2 lbs Brussels sprouts halved

1 block of extra - firm tofu drained and cut into cubes

Salt and pepper to taste

1/3 cup sesame oil

2 Tbsp soy sauce

2 Tbsp rice vinegar

1 tsp oregano

Instructions

1. Preheat oven to 350 F.

2. Clean and cut the Brussels sprouts in halves.

3. Place Brussels sprouts and tofu cubes in a large baking dish.

4. Season evenly with the salt and pepper.

5. Whisk oil, soy sauce, rice vinegar, oregano, and the salt and pepper in a small bowl.

6. Pour the sesame oil mixture evenly over the Brussels sprouts and tofu.

7. Bake for about 30 minutes.

8. Remove from the oven, and allow it to cool down completely.

9. Store in an airtight container for up to 4 days.

Nutrition Facts

Percent daily values based on the Reference Daily Intake (RDI) for a 2000 calorie diet.

Amount Per Serving

Calories 343.37 | Calories From Fat (64%) 220.27 | Total Fat 25.31g 39% | Saturated Fat 3.31g 17% | Cholesterol 0mg 0% | Sodium 464.24mg 19% | Potassium 884.57mg 25% | Total Carbohydrates 21.6g 7% | Fiber 7.14g 29% | Sugar 4.46g | Protein 17,45g 35%

Roasted Pepper Sauce

Ready in Time: 10 minutes | Servings: 6

Ingredients

1 glass roasted peppers, drained and chopped

4 Tbsp olive oil

1 cup finely chopped onion or shallot

3 cloves garlic minced

1/2 cup drained whole canned tomatoes

2 Tbsp chopped fresh parsley

Salt and freshly ground pepper, to taste

Instructions

1. Add all ingredients into a high-speed blender or food processor.

2. Blend until smooth.

3. Store your sauce in a tightly sealed jar or bottle, and keep refrigerated up to two weeks

4. Reheat sauce to be served warm over low heat.

Nutrition Facts

Percent daily values based on the Reference Daily Intake (RDI) for a 2000 calorie diet.

Amount Per Serving

Calories 114.32 | Calories From Fat (71%) 81.1 | Total Fat 9.19g 14% | Saturated Fat 1.27g 6% | Cholesterol 0mg 0% | Sodium 32.14mg 1% | Potassium 207.6mg 6% | Total Carbohydrates 8.15g 3% | Fiber 2.25g 9% | Sugar 1.63g | Protein 1.47g 2%

SIMPLE VEGAN LASAGNA WITH TOFU

Ready in Time: 1 hour and 20 minutes | Servings: 8

Ingredients

For the lasagna:

8 whole vegan grain lasagna noodles

2 Tbs olive oil

1 cup sliced mushrooms

3/4 lb frozen spinach, thawed

1 cup frozen peas, thawed

6 cups marinara sauce

For the tofu spread:

1 1/4 lb extra firm tofu, drained and pressed

1 cup hummus

4 Tbs nutritional yeast

1 tsp garlic powder

1/4 cup fresh basil, finely chopped

Sea salt and ground black pepper

Instructions

1. Preheat oven to 350 F.

2. Place about 1 1/2 cups of marinara sauce in the bottom of a large baking dish; set aside.

3. Cook vegan noodles al dente; drain and rinse with cold water.

4. Heat oil in a large frying skillet over medium heat.

5. Add mushrooms and a pinch of salt and pepper; sauté for 3 to 4 minutes.

6. Add spinach and peas and sauté for further 4 to 5 minutes.

7. Remove pan from the heat.

8. Place drained tofu in a large bowl; crumble with hands.

9. Add hummus, nutritional yeast, basil, salt, and garlic powder.

10. Stir together with your hands until combined well.

11. Top 4 noodles in a prepared baking dish with marinara sauce.

12. Add half of the tofu mixture and half of the vegetable mixture.

13. Top with 1 1/2 cups of marinara sauce.

14. Repeat with more noodles, tofu mixture, and vegetables.

15. Finally, top with one last layer of noodles and all remaining sauce.

16. Sprinkle with nutritional yeast.

17. Cover with foil and bake for 30 minutes.

18. Remove from the oven and allow to cool completely.

19. Cut your lasagna and store in a large airtight container; keep refrigerated up to 4 to 5 days.

20. Or, place your lasagna into heavy-duty freezer bags, and freeze up to one month.

Nutrition Facts

Percent daily values based on the Reference Daily Intake (RDI) for a 2000 calorie diet.

Amount Per Serving

Calories 413.29 | Calories From Fat (29%) 119.48 | Total Fat 13.75g 21% | Saturated Fat 2.12g 11% | Cholesterol 2.57mg <1% | Sodium 750.94mg 31% | Potassium 825.36mg 24% | Total Carbohydrates 55.81g 19% | Fiber 8.6g 35% | Sugar 13g | Protein 19.61g 40%

STUFFED BELL PEPPERS WITH RICE AND PINE NUTS

Ready in Time: 1 hour and 30 minutes | Servings: 8

Ingredients

8 bell peppers (green or red)

1 cup of olive oil

1 large onion finely diced

3 cloves garlic minced

1 large carrot grated

1 cup of rice

1 cup of fresh tomato juice

3 Tbsp semolina flour

Salt and ground pepper to taste

2 Tbsp fresh parsley finely chopped

1 Tbsp fresh basil finely chopped

1 cup pine nuts

1 cup raisins

juice of 2 tomatoes

Instructions

1. Cut the stems of papers and set aside.

2. Remove seeds from peppers and rinse well; set aside to drain.

3. Heat the half of oil in a large frying skillet and sauté the onion, garlic, rice, carrot on high heat.

4. Reduce the heat to moderate, add the tomato, semolina, and the salt and pepper; stir well and remove the pan from the heat.

5. Add the herbs, pine nuts, raisins to the mixture, and stir well.

6. Taste and adjust the salt and ground pepper to taste.

7. Preheat oven to 400 F.

8. Fill the peppers with the rice mixture and cover with their stems or tomato slices.

9. Place stuffed peppers into an oiled baking dish and pour with remaining olive oil and some tomato juice.

10. Bake for about 55 to 60 minutes.

11. Remove from the oven, and let it sit until cool completely.

12. Keep refrigerated in one or two airtight containers up to 4 to 5 days or freeze for up to a month.

Nutrition Facts

Percent daily values based on the Reference Daily Intake (RDI) for a 2000 calorie diet.

Amount Per Serving

Calories 426.48 | Calories From Fat (56%) 238.7 | Total Fat 27.38g 42% | Saturated Fat 3.29g 16% | Cholesterol 0mg 0% | Sodium 93mg 4% | Potassium 605.08mg 17% | Total Carbohydrates 43.86g 15% | Fiber 6.81g 27% | Sugar 12.55g | Protein 5.86g 12%

SWEET RED AND BLACK CHILI WITH CINNAMON

Ready in Time: 45 minutes | Servings: 6

Ingredients

4 Tbs of olive oil

1 onion finely diced

2 cloves garlic, chopped

1 red pepper cut into small cubes

Kosher salt and ground black pepper to taste

1 can (15 oz) red beans, cooked

1 can (11 oz) of black beans

1 can (11 oz) crushed tomatoes

2 tsp chili powder

1/4 tsp ground cinnamon

2 Tbsp fresh parsley finely chopped

2 cups of vegetable broth

Instructions

1. Press the SAUTÉ button on your Instant Pot.

2. When the word "hot" appears on display, add the oil and sauté the onion and garlic with a pinch of salt and pepper until soft; stir occasionally.

3. Add red pepper and stir for one minute.

4. Add red and black beans and stir for one minute.

5. Add all remaining ingredients and give a good stir.

6. Lock lid into place and set on the MANUAL setting high pressure for 20 minutes.

7. When the beep sounds, use the Natural pressure release for 15 minutes.

8. Taste and adjust salt and pepper to taste.

9. Store in an airtight container in the fridge for up to 5 days.

10. Or, let the chili cool a bit, then pack it in a freezer bag or Tupperware container and keep in freezer up to 3 months.

Nutrition Facts

Percent daily values based on the Reference Daily Intake (RDI) for a 2000 calorie diet.

Amount Per Serving

Calories 266.41 | Calories From Fat (34%) 90.97 | Total Fat 10.39g 16% | Saturated Fat 1.58g 8% | Cholesterol 0mg 0% | Sodium 464.62mg 19% | Potassium 686.1mg 20% | Total Carbohydrates 33.73g 11% | Fiber 11.23g 45% | Sugar 4.84g | Protein 12.1g 24%

TUSCAN KALE WITH TAMARI SAUCE

Ready in Time: 15 minutes | Servings: 2

Ingredients

4 cups Tuscan kale

4 Tbsp sesame oil or olive oil

2 tsp Japanese sweet rice wine (or vinegar)

2 Tbsp Tamari sauce

Salt to taste

Instructions

1. Rinse well your kale and cut the bottom side of the stem.

2. Cut kale from top to bottom with the knife.

3. Heat oil in a wok/frying skillet over medium-high heat.

4. Cook kale for about 2 to 3 minutes, stirring frequently.

5. Pour cooking wine (or vinegar) and cook for further one minute.

6. Pour the tamari sauce, stir well and sprinkle with a pinch of salt

7. Cook for a further 2 to 3 minutes or until slightly wilted.

8. Allow cooling completely.

9. Store in an airtight container and keep refrigerated up to 3 to 4 days.

Nutrition Facts

Percent daily values based on the Reference Daily Intake (RDI) for a 2000 calorie diet.

Amount Per Serving

Calories 249.48 | Calories From Fat (96%) 238.3 | Total Fat 27g 42% | Saturated Fat 3.73g 19% | Cholesterol 0mg 0% | Sodium 1006mg 42% | Potassium 38.43mg 1% | Total Carbohydrates 1g <1% | Fiber 0.14g <1% | Sugar 0.31g | Protein 1.9g 4%

Yellow Noodles in Garlic - Hoisin Sauce

Ready in Time: 15 minutes | Servings: 3

Ingredients

20 oz yellow type noodles or spaghetti

Water, for boiling the noodles

Garlic - hoisin sauce

1/2 cup avocado oil

3 Tbsp minced garlic

2 Tbsp hoisin sauce

1 Tbs yellow mustard (without alcohol)

1 Tbs of granulated sugar

Instructions

1. Add yellow noodles into the boiling water and cook for 3 to 4 minutes or until al dente.

2. Transfer the noodles in a colander to drain; set aside.

3. Add all sauce ingredients into saucepan; stir over medium-high heat for about 3 minutes.

4. Transfer warm sauce into a large bowl.

5. Toss noodles into the sauce and toss to combine well.

6. Store in an airtight container and keep refrigerated up to 4 days.

Nutrition Facts

Percent daily values based on the Reference Daily Intake (RDI) for a 2000 calorie diet.

Amount Per Serving

Calories 897.59 | Calories From Fat (26%) 254.28 | Total Fat 28.93g 45% | Saturated Fat 3.55g 18% | Cholesterol 0.32mg <1% | Sodium 244.63mg 10% | Potassium 485.7mg 14% | Total Carbohydrates 154.2g 52% | Fiber 6.77g 27% | Sugar 12.32g | Protein 26.1g 52%

SNACKS

BANANA AND PEANUT BUTTER TORTILLAS

Ready in Time: 15 minutes | Servings: 4

Ingredients

1/3 cup peanut butter

4 medium tortillas

2 large bananas sliced

3 Tbsp peanut oil

Pinch of Kosher salt

Pine Honey for serving (optional)

Instructions

1. Heat a non-stick frying skillet over medium heat.

2. Spread peanut butter over the tortilla.

3. Over half of tortilla arrange the banana slices, sprinkle with a pinch of salt, and top with the remaining tortilla, peanut butter side down.

4. Stick them together and then brush both sides lightly with peanut oil.

5. Place each tortilla in a hot frying pan and cook, flipping once, for about 2 minutes per side.

6. When ready, remove tortillas onto a plate and let cool completely.

7. Cut each tortilla into quarters; store in an airtight container and keep refrigerated up to 5 days.

Nutrition Facts

Percent daily values based on the Reference Daily Intake (RDI) for a 2000 calorie diet.

Amount Per Serving

Calories 371.59 | Calories From Fat (56%) 206.9 | Total Fat 24g 37% | Saturated Fat 3.7g 19% | Cholesterol 0mg 0% | Sodium 302.79mg 13% | Potassium 400.35mg 11% | Total Carbohydrates 34.11g 11% | Fiber 3.82g 15% | Sugar 9.81g | Protein 8.69g 18%

Barbecue Bean Dip (Instant Pot)

Ready in Time: 20 minutes | Servings: 8

Ingredients

1 can (15 oz) cannellini beans rinsed

1 can (6 oz) red beans rinsed and drained

1/2 cup onion finely diced

2 cloves garlic minced

4 Tbsp Barbecue sauce

1/2 cup tomato sauce

3/4 cup vegan ricotta or vegan brie

1 Tbsp fresh parsley chopped

table salt to taste

Instructions

1. Add all ingredients in your Instant Pot.

2. Lock lid into place and set on the MANUAL setting for 15 minutes.

3. When the timer beeps, press "Cancel" and carefully flip the Quick Release valve to let the pressure out.

4. Using an immersion blender, blend the mixture until soft.

5. Transfer dip into the container, and allow to cool down completely.

6. Keep refrigerated up to 5 days.

Nutrition Facts

Percent daily values based on the Reference Daily Intake (RDI) for a 2000 calorie diet.

Amount Per Serving

Calories 297.81 | Calories From Fat (7%) 21.84 | Total Fat 2.5g 4% | Saturated Fat 0.42g 2% | Cholesterol 0mg 0% | Sodium 233.63mg 10% | Potassium 1410.7mg 40% | Total Carbohydrates 50.69g 17% | Fiber 12.19g 49% | Sugar 3.7g | Protein 20.23g 40%

Breaded Cauliflower Florets

Ready in Time: 45 minutes | Servings: 6

Ingredients

1 large head of cauliflower

1 cup rice flour (besan or wheat flour)

1 tsp salt

3/4 tsp garlic powder

3/4 cup water

1 cup chili sauce

2 Tbsp plant butter (any) softened

Instructions

1. Preheat oven to 420 F.

2. Line a large baking sheet with parchment paper; set aside.

3. Rise, clean and cut cauliflower into florets; place in a large bowl.

4. In a separate bowl, combine the rice flour, salt, garlic powder, and water; stir well.

5. Pour the mixture evenly over the cauliflower florets and toss to combine well.

6. Place cauliflower on a prepared baking sheet in a single layer.

7. Place in oven and bake for 15 minutes.

8. In a bowl, whisk together hot sauce and vegetable butter.

9. Transfer the cauliflower to a large bowl.

10. Pour the sauce evenly over cauliflower pieces.

11. Transfer the cauliflower back on the baking sheet and for further 15 minutes.

12. Remove the cauliflower from the oven and set aside to cool down.

13. Refrigerate the cauliflower in an airtight container up to 4 days.

Nutrition Facts

Percent daily values based on the Reference Daily Intake (RDI) for a 2000 calorie diet.

Amount Per Serving

Calories 98.51 | Calories From Fat (29%) 28.58 | Total Fat 3.41g 5% | Saturated Fat 0.31g 2% | Cholesterol 0mg 0% | Sodium 732.57mg 31% | Potassium 375.9mg 11% | Total Carbohydrates 14.43g 5% | Fiber 2.88g 12% | Sugar 2.4g | Protein 4.24g 8%

Coconut- Berry Cream with Turmeric

Ready in Time: 10 minutes | Servings: 4

Ingredients

1 1/2 cups coconut milk canned

1 Tbsp coconut cream softened

1 cup of frozen berries (blueberries, bilberries, raspberries)

1 cup fresh pineapple cut into pieces

1 small banana sliced (frozen or fresh)

1/2 tsp turmeric, freshly grated

2 to 3 Tbsp coconut palm sugar (or granulated sugar)

Instructions

1. Place all ingredients in your fast-speed blender.

2. Blend until smooth and combined well.

3. Taste and adjust sugar to taste.

4. Keep refrigerated in a glass container or jar for up to 5 days.

Nutrition Facts

Percent daily values based on the Reference Daily Intake (RDI) for a 2000 calorie diet.

Amount Per Serving

Calories 252.46 | Calories From Fat (61%) 154.42 | Total Fat 18.5g 28% | Saturated Fat 16.16g 81% | Cholesterol 0mg 0% | Sodium 12.17mg <1% | Potassium 358mg 10% | Total Carbohydrates 24.32g 8% | Fiber 2.19g 9% | Sugar 14.42g | Protein 2.51g 5%

CREAMY EGGPLANT-FLAX DIP

Ready in Time: 20 minutes | Servings: 10

Ingredients

2 eggplants peeled and cut into pieces

1 small onion chopped into small dices

3 Tbsp olive oil

2 clove garlic minced or mashed

1/3 cup of flaxseed flour

1 cup vegetable broth

salt and ground black pepper t to taste

1 cup of vegan mayonnaise

Instructions

1. Peel, rinse and cut eggplant lengthwise into pieces.

2. Add all ingredients (except Mayo) in your Instant Pot; give a good stir.

3. Lock lid into place and set on the MANUAL setting high pressure for 10 minutes.

4. When the beep sounds, quick release the pressure by pressing Cancel, and twisting the steam handle to the Venting position.

5. Remove the mixture into your blender or food processor.

6. Add vegan mayonnaise, and season with the salt and pepper; stir until smooth and creamy.

7. Allow to cool completely, and keep refrigerated in a sealed container up to 5 days.

Nutrition Facts

Percent daily values based on the Reference Daily Intake (RDI) for a 2000 calorie diet.

Amount Per Serving

Calories 223.81 | Calories From Fat (83%) 184.79 | Total Fat 19g 29% | Saturated Fat 1.48g 7% | Cholesterol 0.25mg <1% | Sodium 277.11mg 12% | Potassium 269.6mg 8% | Total Carbohydrates 9.19g 3% | Fiber 3.65g 15% | Sugar 2.68g | Protein 1.69g 3%

ENERGY CAROB STRAWBERRY BARS

Preparation Time: 20 minutes | Servings: 8

Ingredients

1 cup dried dates soaked

1/4 cup carob powder

1/2 cup frozen strawberries

2 scoops vegan protein powder (e.g., chia, soy or hemp)

1/2 cup walnuts chopped

1/4 cup ground flaxseed

1/4 cup sunflower seeds

1/2 tsp lemon zest

1 tsp fresh lemon juice

Sea salt to taste

Instructions

1. Add all ingredients into your food processor.

2. Process until smooth and combined well.

3. Pour the mixture onto a lined baking tray; flat the surface with a knife or spatula.

4. Refrigerate for several hours (at least 4 hours).

5. Remove the mixture from the fridge and cut into bars.

6. Wrap each bar in plastic sheets, and store in an airtight container.

7. Keep refrigerated up to 3 to 4 weeks.

Nutrition Facts

Percent daily values based on the Reference Daily Intake (RDI) for a 2000 calorie diet.

Amount Per Serving

Calories 244 | Calories From Fat (52%) 126.24 | Total Fat 14.63g 23% | Saturated Fat 1.39g 7% | Cholesterol 1.16mg <1% | Sodium 41.6mg 2% | Potassium 301.84mg 9% | Total Carbohydrates 26.6g 9% | Fiber 3.81g 15% | Sugar 15.36g | Protein 5.12g 10%

FRAGRANT SPICED OLIVES

Ready in Time: 10 minutes | Servings: 4

Ingredients

1 tsp coriander seeds crushed

1 Tbsp water

1/2 cup extra-virgin olive oil

3 tsp orange zest

2 tsp garlic finely chopped

1/4 tsp crushed red pepper flakes

2 cups olives pitted (black, green or Kalamata)

1 tsp allspice (ground)

Instructions

1. Add crushed coriander seeds and water into a 1-quart saucepan and cook over medium heat, stirring, for about 1 minute.

2. Add in the olive oil, orange zest, garlic, and red pepper flakes; stir for one minute.

3. Add olives and allspice.

4. Warm your olives, often stirring, about two minutes.

5. Transfer olives to a bowl with liquids, and allow to cool completely.

6. Place olives in an airtight container or jar and keep refrigerated up to one week.

Nutrition Facts

Percent daily values based on the Reference Daily Intake (RDI) for a 2000 calorie diet.

Amount Per Serving

Calories 341.27 | Calories From Fat (92%) 314.6 | Total Fat 35.9g 55% | Saturated Fat 4.9g 24% | Cholesterol 0mg 0% | Sodium 732.71mg 31% | Potassium 26.43mg <1% | Total Carbohydrates 6.57g 2% | Fiber 3.15g 13% | Sugar 0.01g | Protein 1g 2%

FRIED CHICKPEAS CASHEW FRITTERS

Ready in Time: 25 minutes | Servings: 2

Ingredients

1/2 cup cashew halves soaked

1 cup chickpea flour

1/4 tsp turmeric

1/2 tsp red chili powder

1/4 tsp garlic paste

a pinch of baking soda

Salt to taste

2 Tbsp olive oil

water to knead

olive or sesame oil for frying

Instructions

1. Add all ingredients in a food processor; process until combined well.

2. Heat oil in a large non-stick frying skillet.

3. Shape the batter into fritters flatten into little rounds.

4. Fry for about 2 to 3 minutes per side, turning once, or until golden brown.

5. Using a slotted spoon drain onto paper towels., and let sit until cool completely.

6. Store fritters in an airtight container in a dark and cold place for up to one week.

7. Or, refrigerate fritters up to two months.

Nutrition Facts

Percent daily values based on the Reference Daily Intake (RDI) for a 2000 calorie diet.

Amount Per Serving

Calories 576.39 | Calories From Fat (62%) 358.54 | Total Fat 41.58g 64% | Saturated Fat 6.25g 31% | Cholesterol 0mg 0% | Sodium 820.9mg 34% | Potassium 602.94mg 17% | Total Carbohydrates 38.31g 13% | Fiber 6.3g 25% | Sugar 6.6g | Protein 15.7g 32%

GINGER-TURMERIC BUTTERNUT SQUASH CHIPS

Ready in Time: 1 hour and 45 minutes | Servings: 4

Ingredients

1 lb butternut squash cut into 1/8 inch strips

4 Tbsp olive oil

1 tsp ground ginger

1/2 tsp turmeric

1 tsp cinnamon

1/4 tsp nutmeg

pinch salt

Maple syrup for serving (optional)

Instructions

1. Preheat oven to 250 F.

2. Line a baking sheet with parchment paper; set aside.

3. Place the butternut squash strips in a bowl.

4. In a separate bowl, combine all remaining ingredients.

5. Pour the mixture evenly over the butternut squash strips; lightly stir to combine well.

6. Place the butternut slices close to each other on a prepared baking sheet.

7. Bake until crispy or about 90 minutes.

8. When done, let them cool down and store in an air-tight container in the fridge for up to a week.

Nutrition Facts

Percent daily values based on the Reference Daily Intake (RDI) for a 2000 calorie diet.

Amount Per Serving

Calories 171.16 | Calories From Fat (69%) 118.89 | Total Fat 13.8g 21% | Saturated Fat 11.83g 59% | Cholesterol 0mg 0% | Sodium 4.76mg <1% | Potassium 410mg 12% | Total Carbohydrates 13.85g 5% | Fiber 2.54g 10% | Sugar 2.6g | Protein 1.19g 2%

HOMEMADE COCONUT - VANILLA POPCORN

Ready in Time: 25 minutes | Servings: 4

Ingredients

1 cup of unpopped popcorn kernels

3 Tbsp coconut oil melted

2 Tbsp ground almonds

2 tsp pure vanilla extract

2 Tbsp water

Instructions

1. Preheat oven to 350 F.

2. Pop your corn kernels in an air popper or use a microwave oven.

3. Whisk all remaining ingredients in a bowl.

4. Place popcorn in a large and deep bowl, and pour with the coconut oil mixture.

5. Pack the popcorn into an airtight container, and keep on room temperature up to 10 days.

Nutrition Facts

Percent daily values based on the Reference Daily Intake (RDI) for a 2000 calorie diet.

Amount Per Serving

Calories 307.13 | Calories From Fat (41%) 126.13 | Total Fat 14.6g 22% | Saturated Fat 9.32g 47% | Cholesterol 0mg 0% | Sodium 4.04mg <1% | Potassium 170.9mg 5% | Total Carbohydrates 37.74g 13% | Fiber 6.82g 27% | Sugar 0.93g | Protein 6.34g 13%

Oat Biscuits with Seeds

Ready in Time: 30 minutes | Yield: 16 biscuits | Servings: 4

Ingredients

4 Tbsp coconut butter melted

1/2 cup of oatmeal

1/2 cup almond flour

1 tsp baking soda

2 Tbsp sesame seeds

2 tsp poppy seeds

5 to 6 Tbsp of warm water

Instructions

1. Heat oven to 360 F.

2. Grease a large baking sheet and sprinkle with the flour; set aside.

3. Add all ingredients into a bowl, and stir well combine to make a firm dough.

4. Transfer dough onto a lightly floured surface and roll out until getting a thick dough.

5. Cut into small squares and place onto a prepared baking sheet.

6. Bake for about 13 to15 minutes.

7. Remove from the oven, and allow to cool completely.

8. Place biscuits in an airtight container and keep at room temperature up to 2 weeks.

Nutrition Facts

Percent daily values based on the Reference Daily Intake (RDI) for a 2000 calorie diet.

Amount Per Serving

Calories 229.21 | Calories From Fat (68%) 155.1 | Total Fat 17.76g 27% | Saturated Fat 12.38g 62% | Cholesterol 0mg 0% | Sodium 317.12mg 13% | Potassium 115.24mg 3% | Total Carbohydrates 14.37g 5% | Fiber 2.87g 11% | Sugar 0.06g | Protein 4.34g 9%

OLIVE CRACKERS

Preparation Time: 35 minutes | Servings: 16

Ingredients

3/4 cup of flour all-purposes

1 tsp yeast

pinch of salt

1/2 cup of olive oil

1 tsp garlic powder

1/2 cup almond milk

12 black olives finely chopped

1 tsp oregano

2 Tbsp nut cheese (any) crumbled

Instructions

1. Preheat oven to 400 F.

2. Line a baking sheet with parchment paper; set aside.

3. Combine flour, yeast, salt, garlic powder, and almond milk.

4. Stir with a wooden spoon until combined well.

5. Knead the dough by hand until smooth.

6. Form the dough into a ball, wrap in cling film and refrigerate for 2 hours.

7. Take the dough out, fold chopped olives, oregano, and nut cheese; knead lightly.

8. Dust the working surface with flour and roll the dough.

9. Cut the crackers, and arrange on a prepared baking sheet.

10. Bake for 12 to 15 minutes or until golden brown.

11. Store in a sealed container and keep refrigerated for one week.

Nutrition Facts

Percent daily values based on the Reference Daily Intake (RDI) for a 2000 calorie diet.

Amount Per Serving

Calories 138.3 | Calories From Fat (75%) 103.18 | Total Fat 11.86g 18% | Saturated Fat 1.57g 8% | Cholesterol 0mg 0% | Sodium 373.41mg 16% | Potassium 23.3mg <1% | Total Carbohydrates 7.63g 3% | Fiber 1.76g 7% | Sugar 0.08g | Protein 1.27g 3%

Oven-baked Kale-Cashews Chips

Inactive Time: 1 hour | Total Time: 2 hours and 40 minutes | Servings: 6

Instructions

1 cup cashews chopped (soaked)

1 lb fresh kale leaves cut in large pieces

3 Tbsp lemon juice

2 Tbsp water

3 cloves garlic minced

1/3 cup of olive oil

1 tsp red sweet paprika

Pinch of salt

Instructions

1. Soak the cashews in water for at least one hour; drain.

2. Preheat the oven to 200 F.

3. Line a large baking sheet with a foil or parchment paper; set aside.

4. Wash and rinse kale thoroughly and tear the kale in large pieces.

5. Add drained cashews with lemon juice, water, garlic, olive oil, and red paprika in a blender.

6. Blend on HIGH until smooth and combined well.

7. In a large bowl, toss the cashews sauce with kale to combine well

8. Spread the kale leaves evenly on a prepared baking sheet.

9. Bake for 2 1/2 hours, flipping twice.

10. Remove kale chips and allow them to cool down completely.

11. Place kale chips in a zip lock bag and keep refrigerated.

Nutrition Facts

Percent daily values based on the Reference Daily Intake (RDI) for a 2000 calorie diet.

Amount Per Serving

Calories 200.46 | Calories From Fat (73%) 145.57 | Total Fat 16.71g 26% | Saturated Fat 2.55g 13% | Cholesterol 0mg 0% | Sodium 133.25mg 6% | Potassium 422.7mg 12% | Total Carbohydrates 11.2g 4% | Fiber 2g 8% | Sugar 1.13g | Protein 4.2g 8%

PESTO DIP WITH NUTS

Ready in Time: 10 minutes | Servings: 4

Ingredients

1 cup fresh basil leaves, chopped

2 cups zucchini, peeled and chopped

2 cloves garlic minced

1 cup walnuts soaked

1 cup lemon juice from 2 lemons, freshly squeezed

1/2 tsp cumin

Sea salt and black pepper to taste

Instructions

1. Add all ingredients in a high-speed blender; blend until completely smooth.

2. Taste and adjust seasonings to taste.

3. Keep refrigerated in a sealed glass jar for up to one week.

Nutrition Facts

Percent daily values based on the Reference Daily Intake (RDI) for a 2000 calorie diet.

Amount Per Serving

Calories 67.38 | Calories From Fat (64%) 43 | Total Fat 5.14g 8% | Saturated Fat 0.52g 3% | Cholesterol 0mg 0% | Sodium 6.38mg <1% | Potassium 251.75mg 7% | Total Carbohydrates 4.88g 2% | Fiber 1.38g 6% | Sugar 2.18g | Protein 2.39g 5%

Protein Almonds and Carrots Patties

Ready in Time: 15 minutes | Servings: 3

Ingredients

1 cup ground almonds

1/2 cup ground flaxseed

2 large carrots, shredded

2 Tbsp lemon juice, freshly squeezed

3 cloves garlic, finely minced

1 pinch salt and black pepper

3 Tbsp garlic-infused olive oil (or extra-virgin olive oil)

1 scoop vegan protein powder (pea or soy protein)

1 cup water for Instant Pot

Instructions

1. Place all ingredients in a blender and blend until combined well.

2. Shape the mixtures into two or three patties.

3. Pour water to the inner steel pot in the Instant Pot, and place the steamer basket or trivet.

4. Place the patties on the trivet or steamer basket,

5. Lock lid into place and set on the MANUAL setting for 2 minutes.

6. When the timer beeps, press "Cancel" and carefully flip the Quick Release valve to let the pressure out.

7. Once all of the pressure releases, the steam will no longer come out of the vent, and you'll be able to open the lid.

8. Remove patties from the pot, and allow to cool down completely.

9. Place patties in a sealed container, and keep refrigerated up to 5 days.

Nutrition Facts

Percent daily values based on the Reference Daily Intake (RDI) for a 2000 calorie diet.

Amount Per Serving

Calories 434.5 | Calories From Fat (75%) 326.68 | Total Fat 38.23g 59% | Saturated Fat 3.8g 19% | Cholesterol 0.77mg <1% | Sodium 47.45mg 2% | Potassium 545.15mg 16% | Total Carbohydrates 16.72g 6% | Fiber 6.71g 27% | Sugar 5g | Protein 12g 24%

ROASTED CABBAGE WEDGES

Ready in Time: 45 minutes | Servings: 6

Ingredients

1 medium head of cabbage cut into wedges

1/2 cup of extra-virgin olive oil

1 tsp red pepper flakes

2 tsp garlic powder

1 tsp kosher salt or to taste

2 Tbsp fresh lemon juice (2 lemons)

Instructions

1. Preheat oven to 420 F.

2. Line a large baking sheet with foil and brush it with olive oil; set aside.

3. Clean cabbage and remove any damaged outer leaves.

4. Cut it in half, then into quarters and wedges.

5. Place the cabbage wedges in a single layer on the prepared baking sheet.

6. Whisk the olive oil, red pepper flakes, garlic powder, salt, and lemon juice in a bowl.

7. Pour the oil mixture evenly over the cabbage wedges.

8. Bake for 15 minutes, and then flip cabbage and bake for further 15 minutes.

9. Remove from the oven and allow to cool down completely.

10. Store the cabbage wedges in large covered airtight containers up to 4 days.

Nutrition Facts

Percent daily values based on the Reference Daily Intake (RDI) for a 2000 calorie diet.

Amount Per Serving

Calories 201.46 | Calories From Fat (80%) 160.57 | Total Fat 18.17g 28% | Saturated Fat 2.54g 13% | Cholesterol 0mg 0% | Sodium 341.58mg 14% | Potassium 274.8mg 8% | Total Carbohydrates 9.7g 3% | Fiber 3.8g 16% | Sugar 4.5g | Protein 2.12g 4%

Row Pistachio Flaxseed Patties

Ready in Time: 15 minutes | Servings: 2

Ingredients

1 cup pistachio finely sliced

1/2 cup ground flaxseed

2 lemon juice from 2 lemons, freshly squeezed

4 cloves garlic minced or mashed

4 Tbsp olive oil

1 Tbsp fresh parsley finely chopped

1 tsp paprika sweet, powder

salt and black pepper to taste

Instructions

1. Add all ingredients in a food processor.

2. Process until well combined.

3. Shape a mixture into two large or four small patties.

4. Store in an airtight container with parchment paper between each patty.

5. Keep in a fridge for up to two weeks.

Nutrition Facts

Percent daily values based on the Reference Daily Intake (RDI) for a 2000 calorie diet.

Amount Per Serving

Calories 606.94 | Calories From Fat (78%) 473.81 | Total Fat 55.1g 85% | Saturated Fat 7.18g 36% | Cholesterol 0mg 0% | Sodium 3.83mg <1% | Potassium 726.13mg 21% | Total Carbohydrates 23.1g 8% | Fiber 6.7g 27% | Sugar 6.28g | Protein 13.11g 26%

SEASONED SPINACH PATTIES

Ready in Time: 25 minutes | Servings: 6

Ingredients

1/2 lb of spinach cooked

1 small onion

1/2 cup of chickpea flour

3/4 cup almond flour

1/3 cup of olive oil

1 tsp garlic powder

1/4 tsp paprika powder

1/4 tsp turmeric powder

Salt and ground pepper to taste

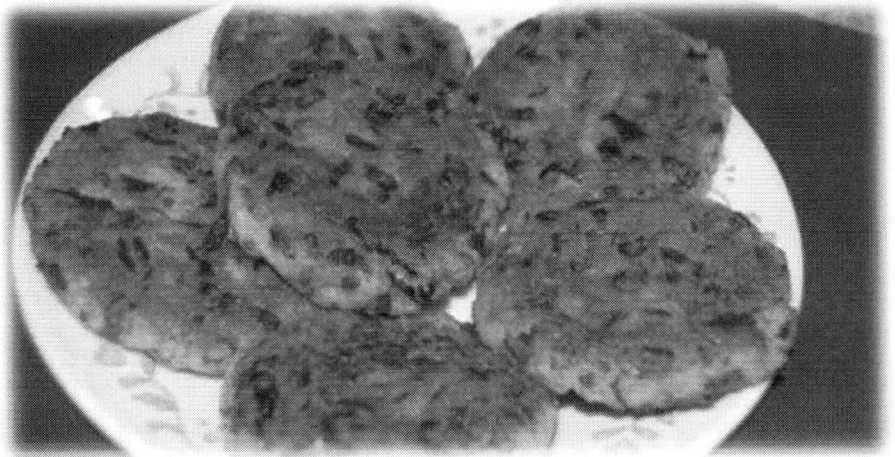

Instructions

1. Boil spinach in salted water for about 5 minutes over medium heat.

2. Remove spinach to a colander, rinse and drain.

3. Place drained spinach along with all remaining ingredients in your high-speed blender or food processor; blend until combined well.

4. Make 6 patties from the mixture and fry in a large frying pan for about 3 minutes per side.

5. Remove patties onto a plate lined with a parchment paper.

6. Keep refrigerated in a sealed container for up to 5 days.

Nutrition Facts

Percent daily values based on the Reference Daily Intake (RDI) for a 2000 calorie diet.

Amount Per Serving

Calories 235.22 | Calories From Fat (49%) 116 | Total Fat 13.19g 20% | Saturated Fat 1.82g 9% | Cholesterol 0mg 0% | Sodium 264mg 11% | Potassium 426.3mg 12% | Total Carbohydrates 22.34g 7% | Fiber 7.65g 31% | Sugar 2g | Protein 9g 18%

SIMPLE SWEET POTATO CHIPS

Ready in Time: 2 hours and 10 minutes | Servings: 4

Ingredients

2 large sweet potatoes

4 Tbsp olive oil

sea salt to taste

Instructions

1. Preheat oven to 250 F.

2. Line a large baking sheet with parchment paper; set aside.

3. Rinse and dry your sweet potatoes thoroughly and slice them very thin; place in a large deep bowl.

4. Sprinkle the sweet potato slices with olive oil and season generously with the salt; toss to combine well.

5. Place in a single layer on a prepared baking sheet.

6. Bake for about 2 hours; flip once at the halfway point.

7. When ready, remove the sweet potatoes from the oven and allow to cool completely.

8. Store the sweet potato chips in an airtight container and keep at a cold and dark place for up to two weeks.

Nutrition Facts

Percent daily values based on the Reference Daily Intake (RDI) for a 2000 calorie diet.

Amount Per Serving

Calories 119.34 | Calories From Fat (78%) 88.34 | Total Fat 13.5g 21% | Saturated Fat 1.86g 9% | Cholesterol 0mg 0% | Sodium 0.27mg <1% | Potassium 0.14mg <1% | Total Carbohydrates 0g 0% | Fiber 0g 0% | Sugar 0g | Protein 0g 0%

Soft Cauliflower and Pecans Spread

Ready in Time: 30 minutes | Servings: 6

Ingredients

1/2 cup of soaked pecans

1 head cauliflower cut into florets

Salt and freshly ground black pepper

3 Tbsp sesame or olive oil

1 onion finely sliced

4 cloves garlic, thinly sliced

1 cup coconut cream

1 sprig thyme chopped

1 tsp tamari sauce

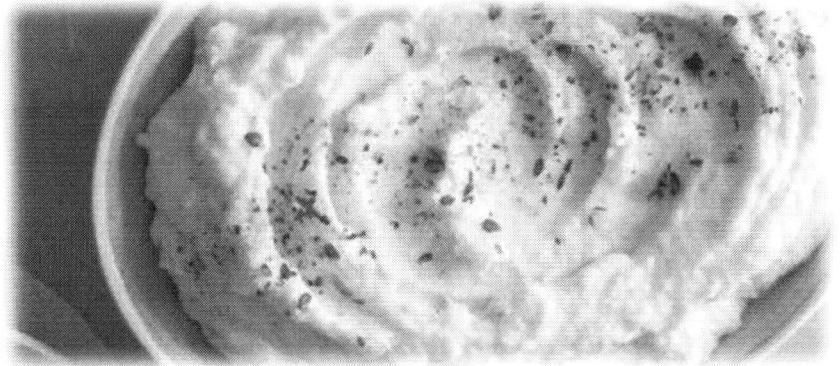

Instructions

1. Soak pecans overnight.

2. Clean cauliflower and divide into florets.

3. Place the cauliflower floret into a large pot and cover with water.

4. Bring to boil and cook for about 6 to 7 minutes over medium-high heat.

5. Remove to a colander and allow it to drain; set aside.

6. In the meantime, heat the oil in a large frying skillet over high heat.

7. Sauté onion and garlic with a pinch of salt for 3 to 4 minutes or until soft.

8. Add cauliflower, pecans, coconut cream, thyme, and tamari sauce; stir for 5 to 6 minutes.

9. Remove from the heat and discard thyme.

10. Using an immersion blender, blend to form a very smooth puree.

11. Season with the salt and pepper to taste.

12. Store into a container and keep refrigerated.

Nutrition Facts

Percent daily values based on the Reference Daily Intake (RDI) for a 2000 calorie diet.

Amount Per Serving

Calories 278,29 | Calories From Fat (84%) 232,44 | Total Fat 27.38g 42% | Saturated Fat 13.7g 69% | Cholesterol 0mg 0% | Sodium 72mg 3% | Potassium 341mg 10% | Total Carbohydrates 8.78g 3% | Fiber 3.12g 12% | Sugar 2.11g | Protein 3.61g 7%

SWEETS/DESSERTS/ENERGYBARS

"RUGGED" COCONUT BALLS

Ready in Time: 15 minutes | Servings: 8

Ingredients

1/3 cup coconut oil melted

1/3 cup coconut butter softened

2 oz coconut, finely shredded, unsweetened

4 Tbsp coconut palm sugar

1/2 cup shredded coconut

Instructions

1. Combine all ingredients in a blender.

2. Blend until soft and well combined.

3. Form small balls from the mixture and roll in shredded coconut.

4. Place on a sheet lined with parchment paper and refrigerate overnight.

5. Keep coconut balls into sealed container in fridge up to one week.

Nutrition Facts

Percent daily values based on the Reference Daily Intake (RDI) for a 2000 calorie diet.

Amount Per Serving

Calories 226.89 | Calories From Fat (84%) 190.39 | Total Fat 21.6g 34% | Saturated Fat 19.84g 99% | Cholesterol 0mg 0% | Sodium 17.19mg <1% | Potassium 45mg 1% | Total Carbohydrates 9g 3% | Fiber 1.16g 5% | Sugar 5.7g | Protein 1g 2%

ALMOND - CHOCO CAKE

Ready in Time: 45 minutes | Servings: 8

Ingredients

1 1/2 cups of almond flour

1/3 cup almonds finely chopped

1/4 cup of cocoa powder unsweetened

Pinch of salt

1/2 tsp baking soda

2 Tbsp almond milk

1/2 cup Coconut oil melted

2 tsp pure vanilla extract

1/3 cup brown sugar (packed)

Instructions

1. Preheat oven to 350 F.

2. Line 9" cake pan with parchment paper, and grease with a little melted coconut oil; set aside.

3. Stir the almond flour, chopped almonds, cocoa powder, salt, and baking soda in a bowl.

4. In a separate bowl, stir the remaining ingredients.

5. Combine the almond flour mixture with the almond milk mixture and stir well.

6. Place batter in a prepared cake pan.

7. Bake for 30 to 32 minutes.

8. Remove from the oven, allow it to cool completely.

9. Store the cake-slices a freezer, tightly wrapped in a double layer of plastic wrap and a layer of foil. It will keep on this way for up to a month.

Nutrition Facts

Percent daily values based on the Reference Daily Intake (RDI) for a 2000 calorie diet.

Amount Per Serving

Calories 195.61 | Calories From Fat (74%) 145.59 | Total Fat 16.9g 26% | Saturated Fat 12.23g 61% | Cholesterol 0mg 0% | Sodium 118.39mg 5% | Potassium 95.64mg 3% | Total Carbohydrates 11.9g 4% | Fiber 1.52g 6% | Sugar 9.35g | Protein 1.75g 4%

BANANA-ALMOND CAKE

Ready in Time: 1 hour | Servings: 8

Ingredients

4 ripe bananas in chunks

3 Tbsš honey or maple syrup

1 tsp pure vanilla extract

1/2 cup almond milk

3/4 cup of self-raising flour

1 tsp cinnamon

1 tsp baking powder

1 pinch of salt

1/3 cup of almonds finely chopped

Almond slices for decoration

Instructions

1. Preheat the oven to 400 F (air mode).

2. Oil a cake mold; set aside.

3. Add bananas into a bowl and mash with the fork.

4. Add honey, vanilla, almond, and stir well.

5. In a separate bowl, stir flour, cinnamon, baking powder, salt, the almonds broken, and mix with a spoon.

6. Combine the flour mixture with the banana mixture, and stir until all ingredients combined well.

7. Transfer the mixture to prepared cake mold and sprinkle with sliced almonds.

8. Bake for 40-45 minutes or until the toothpick inserted comes out clean.

9. Remove from the oven, and allow the cake to cool completely.

10. Cut cake into slices, place in tin foil, or an airtight container, and keep refrigerated up to one week.

Nutrition Facts

Percent daily values based on the Reference Daily Intake (RDI) for a 2000 calorie diet.

Amount Per Serving

Calories 155.94 | Calories From Fat (18%) 27.68 | Total Fat 3.31g 5% | Saturated Fat 0.32g 2% | Cholesterol 0mg 0% | Sodium 98.68mg 4% | Potassium 271mg 8% | Total Carbohydrates 30.61g 10% | Fiber 2.67g 11% | Sugar 14g | Protein 3.6g 7%

Banana-Coconut Ice Cream

Ready in Time: 15 minutes | Servings: 6

Ingredients

1 cup coconut cream

1/2 cup Inverted sugar

2 large frozen bananas (chunks)

3 Tbsp honey extracted

1/4 tsp cinnamon powder

Instructions

1. In a bowl, whip the coconut cream with the inverted sugar.

2. In a separate bowl, beat the banana with honey and cinnamon.

3. Incorporate the coconut whipped cream and banana mixture; stir well.

4. Cover the bowl and let cool in the refrigerator over the night.

5. Stir the mixture 3 to 4 times to avoid crystallization.

6. Keep frozen 1 to 2 months.

Nutrition Facts

Percent daily values based on the Reference Daily Intake (RDI) for a 2000 calorie diet.

Amount Per Serving

Calories 253 | Calories From Fat (46%) 117.23 | Total Fat 14g 22% | Saturated Fat 12.35g 62% | Cholesterol 0mg 0% | Sodium 2.45mg <1% | Potassium 275.25mg 8% | Total Carbohydrates 34.16g 11% | Fiber 1.97g 8% | Sugar 27.19g | Protein 1.91g 4%

Coconut Butter Clouds Cookies

Ready in Time: 25 minutes | Servings: 8

Ingredients

1/2 cup coconut butter softened

1/2 cup peanut butter softened

1/2 cup of granulated sugar

1/2 cup of brown sugar

2 Tbsp chia seeds soaked in 4 tablespoons water

1/2 tsp pure vanilla extract

1/2 tsp baking soda

1/4 tsp salt

1 cup of all-purpose flour

Instructions

1. Preheat oven to 360 F.

2. Add coconut butter, peanut butter, and both sugars in a mixing bowl.

3. Beat with a mixer until soft and sugar combined well.

4. Add soaked chia seeds and vanilla extract; beat.

5. Add baking soda, salt, and flour; beat until all ingredients are combined well.

6. With your hands, shape dough into cookies.

7. Arrange your cookies onto a baking sheet, and bake for about 10 minutes.

8. Remove cookies from the oven and allow to cool completely.

9. Sprinkle with icing sugar and enjoy your cookies.

10. Place cookies in an airtight container and keep refrigerated up to 10 days.

Nutrition Facts

Percent daily values based on the Reference Daily Intake (RDI) for a 2000 calorie diet.

Amount Per Serving

Calories 370.52 | Calories From Fat (50%) 186.69 | Total Fat 21.9g 34% | Saturated Fat 13.5g 68% | Cholesterol 0mg 0% | Sodium 229.6mg 10% | Potassium 140.31mg 4% | Total Carbohydrates 41.1g 14% | Fiber 1.39g 6% | Sugar 27.38g | Protein 5.68g 11%

CHOCOMINT HAZELNUT BARS

Ready in Time: 20 minutes | Servings: 8

Ingredients

1/2 cup coconut oil, melted

4 Tbsp cocoa powder

1/4 cup almond butter

3/4 cup brown sugar - (packed)

1 tsp vanilla extract

1 tsp pure peppermint extract

pinch of salt

1 cup shredded coconut

1 cup hazelnuts sliced

Instructions

1. Chop the hazelnuts in a food processor; set aside.

2. Fill the bottom of a double boiler with water and place it on low heat.

3. Put the coconut oil, cacao powder, almond butter, brown sugar, vanilla, peppermint extract, and salt in the top of a double boiler over hot (not boiling) water and constantly stir for 10 minutes.

4. Add hazelnuts and shredded coconut to the melted mixture and stir together.

5. Pour the mixture in a dish lined with parchment and freeze for several hours.

6. Remove from the freezer and cut into bars.

7. Store in airtight container or freezer bag in a freezer.

8. Let the bars at room temperature for 10 to 15 minutes before eating.

Nutrition Facts

Percent daily values based on the Reference Daily Intake (RDI) for a 2000 calorie diet.

Amount Per Serving

Calories 367.25 | Calories From Fat (66%) 243.32 | Total Fat 28.6g 44% | Saturated Fat 14.37g 72% | Cholesterol 0mg 0% | Sodium 38.33mg 2% | Potassium 253.9mg 7% | Total Carbohydrates 28.58g 10% | Fiber 3.56g 14% | Sugar 23.12g | Protein 4.49g 9%

Coco-Cinnamon Balls

Ready in Time: 15 minutes | Servings: 12

Ingredients

1 cup coconut butter softened

1 cup coconut milk canned

1 tsp pure vanilla extract

3/4 tsp cinnamon

1/2 tsp nutmeg

2 Tbsp coconut palm sugar (or granulated sugar)

1 cup coconut shreds

Instructions

1. Combine all ingredients (except the coconut shreds) in a heated bath - bain-marie.

2. Cook and stir until all ingredients are soft and well combined.

3. Remove bowl from heat, place into a bowl, and refrigerate until the mixture firmed up.

4. Form cold coconut mixture into balls, and roll each ball in the shredded coconut.

5. Store into a sealed container, and keep refrigerated up to one week.

Nutrition Facts

Percent daily values based on the Reference Daily Intake (RDI) for a 2000 calorie diet.

Amount Per Serving

Calories 225.6 | Calories From Fat (93%) 209.22 | Total Fat 24.5g 38% | Saturated Fat 21.28g 106% | Cholesterol 0mg 0% | Sodium 3.84mg <1% | Potassium 66.71mg 2% | Total Carbohydrates 3.5g 1% | Fiber 0.71g 3% | Sugar 1.68g | Protein 0.61g 1%

EXPRESS COCONUT FLAX PUDDING

Ready in Time: 15 minutes | Servings: 4

Ingredients

1 Tbsp coconut oil softened

1 Tbsp coconut cream

2 cups coconut milk canned

3/4 cup ground flax seed

4 Tbsp coconut palm sugar (or to taste)

Instructions

1. Press SAUTÉ button on your Instant Pot

2. Add coconut oil, coconut cream, coconut milk, and ground flaxseed.

3. Stir about 5 - 10 minutes.

4. Lock lid into place and set on the MANUAL setting for 5 minutes.

5. When the timer beeps, press "Cancel" and carefully flip the Quick Release valve to let the pressure out.

6. Add the palm sugar and stir well.

7. Taste and adjust sugar to taste.

8. Allow pudding to cool down completely.

9. Place the pudding in an airtight container and refrigerate for up to 2 weeks.

Nutrition Facts

Percent daily values based on the Reference Daily Intake (RDI) for a 2000 calorie diet.

Amount Per Serving

Calories 446.5 | Calories From Fat (75%) 334.39 | Total Fat 39.4g 61% | Saturated Fat 25.46g 127% | Cholesterol 0mg 0% | Sodium 23.42mg <1% | Potassium 485.7mg 14% | Total Carbohydrates 21.9g 7% | Fiber 7.94g 32% | Sugar 7.6g | Protein 7.61g 15%

Full-flavored Vanilla Ice Cream

Ready in Time: 15 minutes | Servings: 8

Ingredients

1 1/2 cups canned coconut milk

1 cup coconut whipping cream

1 frozen banana cut into chunks

1 cup vanilla sugar

3 Tbsp apple sauce

2 tsp pure vanilla extract

1 tsp Xanthan gum or agar-agar thickening agent

Instructions

1. Add all ingredients in a food processor; process until all ingredients combined well.

2. Place the ice cream mixture in a freezer-safe container with a lid over.

3. Freeze for at least 4 hours.

4. Remove frozen mixture to a bowl and beat with a mixer to break up the ice crystals.

5. Repeat this process 3 to 4 times.

6. Let the ice cream at room temperature for 15 minutes before serving.

Nutrition Facts

Percent daily values based on the Reference Daily Intake (RDI) for a 2000 calorie diet.

Amount Per Serving

Calories 238.47 | Calories From Fat (68%) 163.29 | Total Fat 19.51g 30% | Saturated Fat 17.26g 86% | Cholesterol 0mg 0% | Sodium 8.24mg <1% | Potassium 268.5mg 8% | Total Carbohydrates 8.8g 3% | Fiber 1.1g 4% | Sugar 4.12g | Protein 2.12g 4%

IRRESISTIBLE PEANUT COOKIES

Ready in Time: 25 minutes | Servings: 8

Ingredients

4 Tbsp all-purpose flour

1 tsp baking soda

pinch of salt

1/3 cup granulated sugar

1/3 cup peanut butter softened

3 Tbsp applesauce

1/2 tsp pure vanilla extract

Instructions

1. Preheat oven to 350 F.

2. Combine the flour, baking soda, salt, and sugar in a mixing bowl; stir.

3. Add all remaining ingredients and stir well to form a dough.

4. Roll dough into cookie balls/patties.

5. Arrange your cookies onto greased (with oil or cooking spray) baking sheet.

6. Bake for about 8 to 10 minutes.

7. Let cool for at least 15 minutes before removing from tray.

8. Remove cookies from the tray and let cool completely.

9. Place your peanut butter cookies in an airtight container, and keep refrigerated up to 10 days.

Nutrition Facts

Percent daily values based on the Reference Daily Intake (RDI) for a 2000 calorie diet.

Amount Per Serving

Calories 112.39 | Calories From Fat (42%) 46.73 | Total Fat 5.58g 9% | Saturated Fat 1.15g 6% | Cholesterol 0mg 0% | Sodium 206.8mg 9% | Potassium 82.81mg 2% | Total Carbohydrates 13.82g 5% | Fiber 0.84g 3% | Sugar 9.93g | Protein 3.1g 6%

MURKY ALMOND COOKIES

Ready in Time: 25 minutes | Servings: 12

Ingredients

4 Tbsp cocoa powder

2 cups almond flour

1/4 tsp salt

1/2 tsp baking soda

5 Tbsp coconut oil melted

2 Tbsp almond milk

1 1/2 tsp almond extract

1 tsp vanilla extract

4 Tbsp corn syrup or honey

Instructions

1. Preheat oven to 340 F degrees.

2. Grease a large baking sheet; set aside.

3. Combine the cocoa powder, almond flour, salt, and baking soda in a bowl.

4. In a separate bowl, whisk melted coconut oil, almond milk, almond and vanilla extract, and corn syrup or honey.

5. Combine the almond flour mixture with the almond milk mixture and stir until all ingredients incorporate well.

6. Roll tablespoons of the dough into balls, and arrange onto a prepared baking sheet.

7. Bake for 12 to 15 minutes.

8. Remove from the oven and transfer onto a plate lined with a paper towel.

9. Allow cookies to cool down completely and store in an airtight container at room temperature for about four days.

Nutrition Facts

Percent daily values based on the Reference Daily Intake (RDI) for a 2000 calorie diet.

Amount Per Serving

Calories 78.31 | Calories From Fat (68%) 53.17 | Total Fat 5.94g 9% | Saturated Fat 5.48g 27% | Cholesterol 0.2mg <1% | Sodium 39.62mg 2% | Potassium 35.27mg 1% | Total Carbohydrates 6.8g 2% | Fiber 0.61g 2% | Sugar 5.5g | Protein 0.46g <1%

Orange Semolina Halva

Ready in Time: 35 minutes | Servings: 12

Ingredients

6 cups fresh orange juice

Zest from 3 oranges

3 cups brown sugar

1 1/4 cup semolina flour

1 Tbsp almond butter (plain, unsalted)

4 Tbsp ground almond

1/4 tsp cinnamon

Instructions

1. Heat the orange juice, orange zest with brown sugar in a pot.

2. Stir over medium heat until sugar is dissolved.

3. Add the semolina flour and cook over low heat for 15 minutes; stir occasionally.

4. Add almond butter, ground almonds, and cinnamon, and stir well.

5. Cook, frequently stirring, for further 5 minutes.

6. Transfer the halva mixture into a mold, let it cool and refrigerate for at least 4 hours.

7. Keep refrigerated in a sealed container for one week.

Nutrition Facts

Percent daily values based on the Reference Daily Intake (RDI) for a 2000 calorie diet.

Amount Per Serving

Calories 352.85 | Calories From Fat (6%) 22.34 | Total Fat 2.67g 4% | Saturated Fat 0.23g 1% | Cholesterol 0mg 0% | Sodium 17mg <1% | Potassium 384.18mg 11% | Total Carbohydrates 80.42g 27% | Fiber 1.41g 6% | Sugar 63.8g | Protein 4.03g 8%

SEASONED CINNAMON MANGO POPSICLES

Ready in Time: 15 minutes | Servings: 6

Ingredients

1 1/2 cups of mango pulp

1 mango cut in cubes

1 cup brown sugar (packed)

2 Tbsp lemon juice freshly squeezed

1 tsp cinnamon

1 pinch of salt

Instructions

1. Add all ingredients into your blender.

2. Blend until brown sugar dissolved.

3. Pour the mango mixture evenly in popsicle molds or cups.

4. Insert sticks into each mold.

5. Place molds in a freezer, and freeze for at least 5 to6 hours.

6. Before serving, un-mold easy your popsicles placing molds under lukewarm water.

Nutrition Facts

Percent daily values based on the Reference Daily Intake (RDI) for a 2000 calorie diet.

Amount Per Serving

Calories 166.47 | Calories From Fat (1%) 1.47 | Total Fat 0.18g <1% | Saturated Fat 0.04g <1% | Cholesterol 0mg 0% | Sodium 59.22mg 2% | Potassium 125.5mg 4% | Total Carbohydrates 42.9g 14% | Fiber 1g 4% | Sugar 41.39g | Protein 0.42g <1%

Strawberry Molasses Ice Cream

Ready in Time: 20 minutes | Servings: 8

Ingredients

1 lb strawberries

3/4 cup coconut palm sugar (or granulated sugar)

1 cup coconut cream

1 Tbsp molasses

1 tsp balsamic vinegar

1/2 tsp agar-agar

1/2 tsp pure strawberry extract

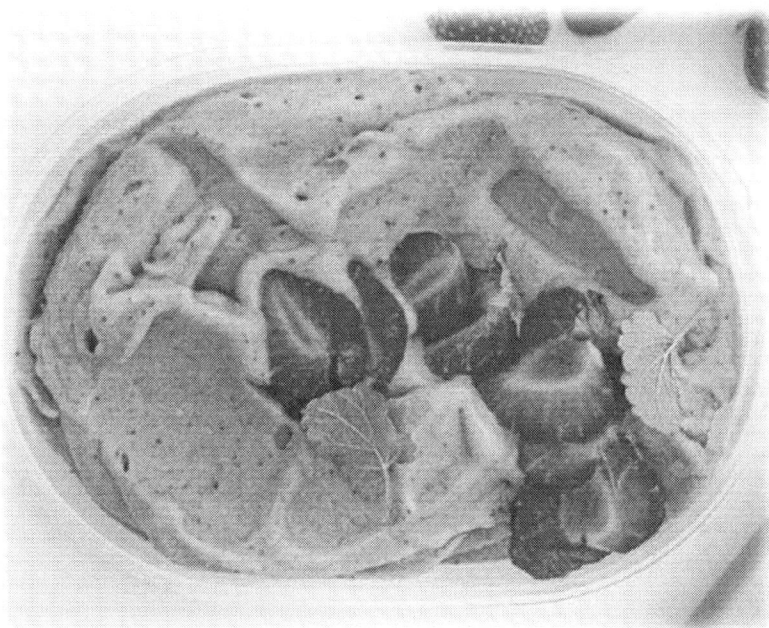

Instructions

1. Add strawberries, date sugar, and
the balsamic vinegar in a blender; blend until completely combined.

2. Place the mixture in the refrigerator for one hour.

3. In a mixing bowl, beat the coconut cream with an electric mixer to make a thick mixture.

4. Add molasses, balsamic vinegar, agar-agar, and beat for further one minute or until combined well.

5. Add the strawberry mixture and beat again for 2 minutes.

6. Pour ice cream mix into an ice cream maker, turn on the machine, and churn according to manufacturer's directions.

7. Keep frozen in a freezer-safe container (with plastic film and lid over).

Nutrition Facts

Percent daily values based on the Reference Daily Intake (RDI) for a 2000 calorie diet.

Amount Per Serving

Calories 184.23 | Calories From Fat (48%) 88.3 | Total Fat 10.58g 16% | Saturated Fat 9.23g 46% | Cholesterol 0mg 0% | Sodium 2.87mg <1% | Potassium 221.8mg 6% | Total Carbohydrates 23g 8% | Fiber 1.9g 7% | Sugar 15g | Protein 1.47g 3%

Strawberry-Mint Sorbet

Ready in Time: 15 minutes | Servings: 6

Ingredients

1 cup of granulated sugar

1 cup of orange juice

1 lb frozen strawberries

1 tsp pure peppermint extract

Instructions

1. Add sugar and orange juice in a saucepan.

2. Stir over high heat and boil for 5 minutes or until sugar dissolves.

3. Remove from the heat and let it cool down.

4. Add strawberries into a blender, and blend until smooth.

5. Pour syrup into strawberries, add peppermint extract and stir until all ingredients combined well.

6. Transfer mixture to a storage container, cover tightly, and freeze until ready to serve.

Nutrition Facts

Percent daily values based on the Reference Daily Intake (RDI) for a 2000 calorie diet.

Amount Per Serving

Calories 167.86 | Calories From Fat (1%) 1.15 | Total Fat 0.14g <1% | Saturated Fat 0.01g <1% | Cholesterol 0mg 0% | Sodium 2.12mg <1% | Potassium 167.7mg 5% | Total Carbohydrates 43g 14% | Fiber 1.64g 7% | Sugar 39g | Protein 0.52g 1%

VEGAN CHOCO - HAZELNUT SPREAD

Ready in Time: 15 minutes | Servings: 6

Ingredients

1 cup hazelnuts soaked

4 Tbsp dry cacao powder

4 Tbsp Maple syrup

1 tsp pure vanilla extract

1/4 tsp Kosher salt

4 Tbsp almond milk

Instructions

1. Soak hazelnuts with water overnight.

2. Add soaked hazelnuts along with all remaining ingredients in a food processor.

3. Process for about 10 minutes or until a cream get the desired consistency.

4. Keep the spread in a sealed container refrigerated up to 2 weeks.

Nutrition Facts

Percent daily values based on the Reference Daily Intake (RDI) for a 2000 calorie diet.

Amount Per Serving

Calories 289 | Calories From Fat (70%) 201.61 | Total Fat 24g 37% | Saturated Fat 2g 10% | Cholesterol 0mg 0% | Sodium 80.75mg 3% | Potassium 369.56mg 11% | Total Carbohydrates 17.6g 6% | Fiber 4.75g 19% | Sugar 10g | Protein 6,39g 13%

VEGAN EXOTIC CHOCOLATE MOUSSE

Ready in Time: 10 minutes | Servings: 5

Instructions

2 frozen bananas chunks

2 avocados

1/3 cup of dates

4 Tbsp cocoa powder

1/2 cup of fresh orange juice

zest, from 1 orange

Instructions

1. Add bananas, avocado, and dates in a food processor.

2. Process for about 2 to 3 minutes until combined well.

3. Add cocoa powder, orange juice, and orange zest; process for further one minute.

4. Place cream in a glass jar or container and keep refrigerated up to one week.

Nutrition Facts

Percent daily values based on the Reference Daily Intake (RDI) for a 2000 calorie diet.

Amount Per Serving

Calories 213.56 | Calories From Fat (45%) 96.53 | Total Fat 11.51g 18% | Saturated Fat 1.88g 9% | Cholesterol 0mg 0% | Sodium 7.5mg <1% | Potassium 716.42mg 20% | Total Carbohydrates 31.13g 10% | Fiber 8.53g 34% | Sugar 15.65g | Protein 3.21g 6%

Vegan Lemon Pudding

Ready in Time: 20 minutes | Servings: 3

Ingredients

2 cups almond milk

3 Tbsp of cornflour

2 Tbsp of all-purpose flour

1 cup of sugar granulated

1/4 cup almond butter (plain, unsalted)

1 tsp lemon zest

1/3 cup fresh lemon juice

Instructions

1. Add the almond milk with cornflour, flour, and sugar in a saucepan.

2. Cook, frequently stirring, until sugar dissolved, and all ingredients combine well (for about 5 to 7 minutes over medium heat).

3. Add the almond butter, lemon zest, and lemon juice.

4. Cook, frequently stirring, for further 5 to 6 minutes.

5. Remove the lemon pudding from the heat and allow it to cool completely.

6. Pour into the sealed container and keep refrigerated up to one week.

Nutrition Facts

Percent daily values based on the Reference Daily Intake (RDI) for a 2000 calorie diet.

Amount Per Serving

Calories 178.8 | Calories From Fat (52%) 93.14 | Total Fat 11.5g 18% | Saturated Fat 0.92g 5% | Cholesterol 0mg 0% | Sodium 2.21mg <1% | Potassium 208.57mg 6% | Total Carbohydrates 18.58g 6% | Fiber 2.86g 11% | Sugar 1.63g | Protein 5.7g 12%

Vitamin Blast Tropical Sherbet

Preparation Time: 15 minutes | Servings: 10

Ingredients

4 cups mangos pitted and cut into 1/2-inch dice

1 papaya cut into 1/2-inch dice

1/4 cup granulated sugar or honey (optional)

1 cup pineapple juice canned

1/4 cup coconut milk

2 Tbsp coconut cream

1 fresh lime juice

Instructions

1. Add all ingredients into your food processor; process until all ingredients smooth and combine well.

2. Transfer the mixture to a bowl, cover, and refrigerate for about 2 hours.

3. Remove the sherbet mixture from the fridge, stir well, and pour in a freezer-safe container (with plastic film and lid over).

4. Keep frozen.

5. Let the sherbet at room temperature for 15 minutes before serving.

Nutrition Facts

Percent daily values based on the Reference Daily Intake (RDI) for a 2000 calorie diet.

Amount Per Serving

Calories 104.15 | Calories From Fat (16%) 16.96 | Total Fat 2g 3% | Saturated Fat 1.5g 8% | Cholesterol 0mg 0% | Sodium 3mg <1% | Potassium 214.95mg 6% | Total Carbohydrates 22.54g 8% | Fiber 1.68g 7% | Sugar 17.2g | Protein 1.2g 2%

WALNUT VANILLA POPSICLES

Ready in Time: 15 minutes | Servings: 8

Ingredients

1 1/2 cup finely sliced walnuts

4 cups of almond milk

4 Tbsp brown sugar (packed)

1 scoop protein powder (pea or soy)

2 tsp pure vanilla extract

Instructions

1. Add all ingredients in your high-speed blender and blend until smooth and combined well.

2. Pour the mixture in popsicle molds and insert the wooden stick into the middle of each mold.

3. Freeze until your ice popsicles are completely frozen.

4. Serve and enjoy!

Nutrition Facts

Percent daily values based on the Reference Daily Intake (RDI) for a 2000 calorie diet.

Amount Per Serving

Calories 212.59 | Calories From Fat (69%) 147.22 | Total Fat 16.7g 26% | Saturated Fat 1.4g 7% | Cholesterol 0.05mg <1% | Sodium 142.8mg 6% | Potassium 108.2mg 3% | Total Carbohydrates 11.47g 4% | Fiber 1.47g 6% | Sugar 7.46g | Protein 4.37g 9%

ABOUT THE AUTHOR

Joseph P. Turner has spent his life learning what makes a healthy lifestyle and how to train our bodies to achieve maximum potential. What makes his journey more incredible is he has learned how to do all this while being vegan. He believes that we can each achieve optimum health without compromising our core values and maintaining a healthy lifestyle without the chemicals and preservatives that go into most good. His healthy living approach is both simple and easy to maintain.

His first book is the Meatless Power Cookbook for Vegan Athletes. It focuses on his own personal recipes as well as several he has discovered over the years to trim the fat, lose weight, and feel good in the process.

Joseph is a certified fitness trainer and nutritionist. When he is not in the gym Joseph can be found hard at work in the kitchen whipping up his favorite meals or creating new, delicious dishes. Writing may be his latest endeavor, but cooking has always been his true passion.

YOUR FREE GIFT

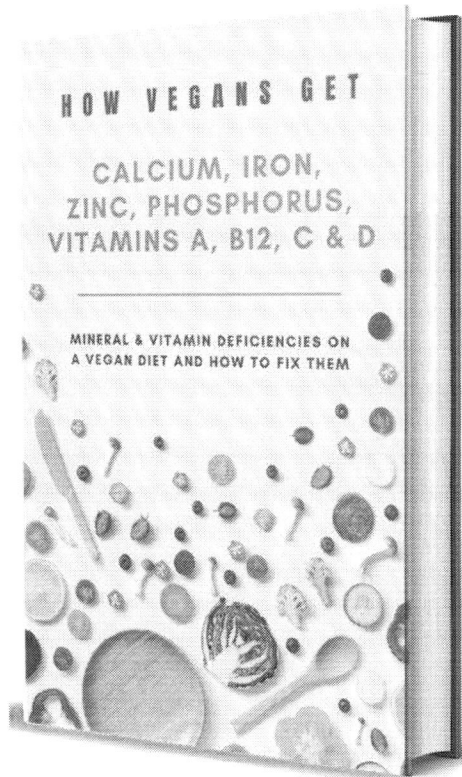

LINK ON THE BOOK: *BIT.LY/VEGAN-BONUS-BOOK* OR SCAN QR CODE BELOW

OTHER BOOKS BY JOSEPH P. TURNER

MEATLESS POWER COOKBOOK FOR VEGAN ATHLETES

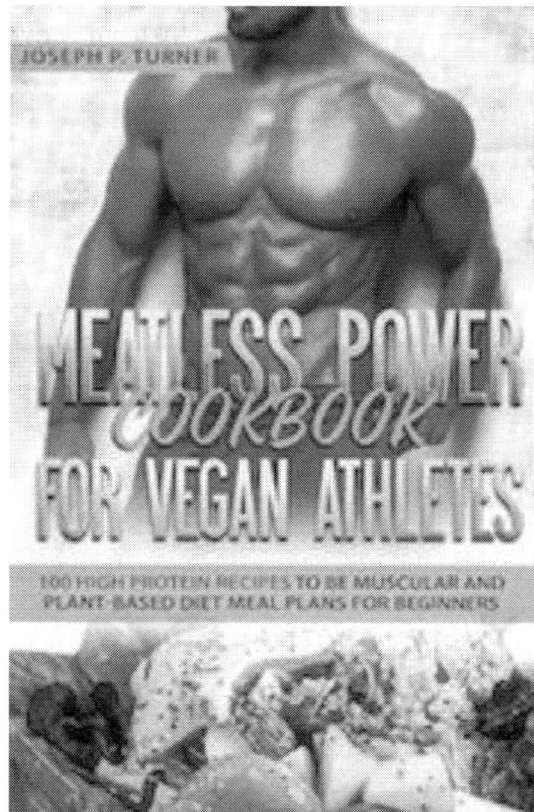

https://geni.us/vegan-athletes

ONE LAST THING...

DID YOU ENJOY THE BOOK?

IF SO, THEN LET ME KNOW BY LEAVING A REVIEW ON AMAZON! Reviews are the lifeblood of independent authors. I would appreciate even a few words and rating if that's all you have time for

IF YOU DID NOT LIKE THIS BOOK, THEN PLEASE TELL ME! Email me at perfectecruz@gmail.com and let me know what you didn't like! Perhaps I can change it. In today's world, a book doesn't have to be stagnant; it can improve with time and feedback from readers like you. You can impact this book, and I welcome your feedback. Help make this book better for everyone!

Printed in Great Britain
by Amazon